the ten demandments

Rules to Live by in the Age of the Demanding Customer

the ten demandments

Rules to Live by in the Age of the Demanding Customer

KELLY MOONEY
WITH LAURA BERGHEIM

Library of Congress Cataloging-in-Publication Data

Mooney, P. Kelly.
 The ten demandments / by P. Kelly Mooney with Laura Bergheim.
     p. cm.
Includes index.
 ISBN 0-07-138739-0 (hardcover : alk. Paper)
1. Customer relations. 2. Customer services. 3. Customer loyalty
4. Consumer satisfaction. I. Bergheim, Laura, 1962- II. Title.
 HF5415.5 .M66 2002
 658.8'12—dc21

                              2002003898

          2 3 4 5 6 7 8 9 0 AGM / AGM 0 9 8 7 6 5 4 3 2

ISBN 0-07-138739-0

Printed and bound by Quebecor Martinsburg.

McGraw-Hill books are available at special quantity to use as premiums and sales promotions, or for use in corporate training programs. For more information, please write to the Director of Special Sales, Professional Publishing, McGraw-Hill, Two Penn Plaza, New York, NY 10121-2298. Or contact your local bookstore.

 This book is printed on recycled, acid-free paper containing a minimum of 50% recycled, de-inked fiber.

To my darling
angels, Luke and Riley, who are
daily reminders of what's most
important in life.

contents

acknowledgments

THIS BOOK IS LARGELY A PRODUCT of what my colleagues and I at Ten Worldwide and its member companies have observed, learned, and discovered by helping some of the country's leading brands satisfy some of the world's most demanding consumers. I feel privileged to have worked with progressive clients that have exposed me to both the challenges and the rewards of building a seamless, customer-centric organization.

Nancy Kramer, Ten Worldwide's CEO, has provided unrelenting support and encouragement since the day I called her from a Fast Company conference with the idea for this book. She and her part-

ACKNOWLEDGMENTS

ners enthusiastically agreed to allow me to devote time to this initiative while running Ten/Resource, the interactive marketing company of Ten Worldwide. Christopher Celeste, my former boss and mentor, encouraged me to actually write this book, and not merely to dream about it. I thank him for being a coach and sounding board, and for continually adding new ideas that made this book stronger.

Every associate who contributed to the consumer studies that made up the Resource E-commerce Watch™ series played a significant role in developing some of this book's core themes over the last few years. The work would have suffered without the sheer brilliance, strategic insight, and consumer behavior savvy of Jenny Barrett, Edd Johns, and Susan Ashley. In addition, I thank my colleagues who kept the ship afloat, taking things off my plate while I was distracted, including Dana Ellis, Laura Evans, Robin Butler, and Dennis Bajec.

When I decided to write this book, I quickly turned to some seasoned pros, who graciously shared their experiences with me. Roger Blackwell, Steve Strasser, Frank Pacetta, Robin Baliszewski, Mark Willis, Ed Trolley, Keriake Lucas, Caroline Cofer, and Debbie Phillips all provided me with expertise that would have taken me years otherwise to acquire on my own. All those folks and the resourcefulness of Betsy Davis led me to my agent, Karen Watts, who believed in me from day one, despite the fact that I had initially intended to write a digital book (!). And a genuine thanks goes to Mary Glenn and the rest of the McGraw-Hill team for their unwavering dedication to the success of this book.

I also want to thank the many people who let me interrupt their busy schedules so that I could develop a better understanding of their challenges in meeting the expectations of today's increasingly sophisticated, less tolerant consumers. Leaders from top companies including The Limited, Progressive Insurance, Liz Claiborne, Procter & Gamble, Hershey's, House of Blues, RedEnvelope, Krispy Kreme, Starbucks, Kinko's, TH!NK Mobility, UncommonGoods, Hewlett-Packard, and Reflect.com offered insights for delivering a great total experience.

Keen minds and creative talent throughout our organization were tapped; I owe a special thanks, however, to Christopher Barcelona as the creative force that pushed me and McGraw-Hill to create a business book that stands out from the pack and visually represents the unique tone of the narrative. Photography was an important part of communicating each of the Ten Demandments, made possible on a shoestring budget with the additional help of Lynn Sampson, Scott Heidelberg, and Steve Chieffo.

The people in the photographs are exactly that. People. Not actors. They're friends, relatives, and acquaintances who helped me to tell the story. For giving up personal time over a weekend, not to mention agreeing to use of their image, I thank James Scott, Kristen Polk, Bill Mooney (my dad!), Christopher Celeste, Alan Moser, Tessa Dillon, John El Amin, Peggy Miller, Kelly Wright, Dave Barber, Jackie Keagy, and Robert Mora.

There were many friends and colleagues who reviewed or participated in reading, editing, and commenting on the manuscript during its various stages, including Kate Murphy, Bob Hale, Lisa Cook, Shelagh Wright, Gregor Gilliom, James Scott, Jenny Barrett, Aaron Spiess, Lisa Bownas, Shawn Wolfe, and Katy Mooney. I thank all of them for their candid and constructive advice.

This project would have stalled without the many talents of Karen Scholl, who served as Research Director for this book. Her highly attuned skills for discovering the gem of an insight or thread of a theme buried within a pile of studies, articles, or Web pages is remarkable. She not only managed the project and its reams of research but also arranged for executive interviews, strengthened the manuscript with her edits and writing assistance, and helped to shape the self-evaluations at the end of each chapter.

More than anyone else, my colleague and co-author Laura Bergheim helped to bring this book to life. Her gift for language combined with her passionate quest for learning about consumer behavior, absorbing cultural trends, and telling stories, is unmatched. Not only was she able to devote her expertise to this book but, having been published, she willingly shepherded me through this process, resulting in surprising efficiencies and an end product that we're both proud of. For her unyielding dedication, I am forever grateful.

And last, my undying thanks to my devoted husband and life-partner, Scott Henningsen, who patiently managed our family life, and particularly meal times, while this manuscript was being born.

preface

WHEN I STARTED OUT TO write about what consumers really
wanted—and demanded—from companies, I was going to write
about delivering a killer customer experience on the Web. Okay, so
now I know that book would have joined the ranks of all the other
dot-com dust-collectors from that bygone, bubble-burst era.

But I knew that what I had learned during my years of examining
and critiquing the best and brightest and worst and dimmest online
experiences also translated to the wider world. I realized that it was
immaterial where companies were delivering the best experiences to
consumers—it only mattered if they were.

For most companies (with the exception of the few remaining "pure players"), the Internet has become not a new business, but rather a thread for weaving together divisions and product lines, reaching out in more dynamic ways to customer segments, and enhancing and supporting the brand experience in every channel, online or off.

So the Web isn't the be-all, end-all delivery system for consumer experiences. But it has certainly made consumers sit up and take notice by giving them a lot of stuff they never really got before—like more customized experiences, deeper product information, and more selection than any mall could match—and now they want those things and more, everywhere they experience a brand. The Internet has, in essence, empowered them to take control of their consumer experiences as never before.

Companies that hope to earn consumer trust and loyalty need to understand what is expected of them in this new age of the demanding consumer.

With all of this in mind, I decided to write a different book. One that's not about the Internet in and of itself, or target marketing, or customer relationship management (CRM) technologies. Instead I chose to write about people and their needs from the companies they keep. Healthy relationships. Inspiring experiences. Common courtesies. Genuine respect. And real empowerment.

I wanted to hold a mirror up to companies so they could see themselves as their customers see them, and I wanted to make them walk a mile in the shoes of the folks standing on the other side of the counter or sitting at the other end of the mouse.

The book you hold in your hands is a manifesto that reflects the mind-set of today's demanding consumers, who shake their heads (and sometimes their fists) at the companies that still don't get it. Along the way, the book also strives to show how and why consumers are giving their trust, business, and eventual loyalty to the companies that do right by them.

My mission is to get companies to pack up their campaigns of persuasion, toss out their wasteful junk mail, energize their apathetic sales associates, and wipe out their prehistoric policies. I want to inspire and compel them to nurture and propagate a customer religion within their organization—one that permeates widely and deeply throughout every nook and cranny, from the boardroom to the mailroom.

I wrote this book because I had to—not that I have that much spare time, what with being a wife, the mother of two young kids, and running a company!—because I'm on a mission to give consumers a real voice and companies a real wake-up call.

Still, I know that no one really *needs* to write a book—much less one about how to be consumer-centric. You can't pick up a newspaper business section, trade publication, or new economy marketing book without getting that same message loud and clear. But if the message is being sent, why isn't it being received yet?

As a consumer, not as a business leader or consultant, why do I routinely feel let down, frustrated, and compromised by my experiences with companies? Why am I still plagued by long waits on toll-free calls, mistreated by customer service associates, and disappointed by lackluster products, even after I've given companies all the info they've asked for about my preferences and needs?

Let me tell you right now, I'm probably disappointed more often than I'm delighted by my experiences with most brands, though I've learned to stay loyal to the companies that get it, and to avoid those that don't. But still—my tolerance is decreasing day by day. And I know I'm not alone!

I sometimes feel like I'm perpetually staging a personal boycott, refusing to give my business to a company that has appalled me. I'll steer clear of the nearby Italian restaurant that's botched my take-out order three times in a row. And I'll avoid the most convenient coffee shop to my office because the service is so surly I'm made to feel like a pest just for requesting extra cream. Yet these companies seem unaware of my absence, because, well, it's invisible, and so they're utterly unaware of how my lost business is hitting their bottom line.

Doesn't it make you wonder: If we're all harboring personal boycotts in our daily lives, how many millions of missed opportunities are bedeviling oblivious companies? If they could see the impact of all the business they've lost because of consumer disgruntlement, I'm betting they'd take notice—and take action.

I know there are a lot of really great companies out there that work hard to please their consumers and deliver quality experiences, and I've interviewed executives from many of them for this book. But setting that cream of the crop aside, I'm convinced that most companies simply haven't cultivated a consumer-first culture. And it baffles me that they haven't—because without their consumers, they can't survive.

Many companies don't operate from a shared understanding of who their consumers are (and who they aren't). They don't know what their consumers want or expect from their experience with a brand. They haven't developed a perspective on how to permeate their organization with consumer-centric thinking. And they haven't laid down a foundational set of rules to live and die by that provides the building blocks of consumer loyalty. So that's what I've done for them, by honoring the voice that's seldom heard inside the corporate headquarters. The voice of the consumer.

THE GENESIS OF *THE TEN DEMANDMENTS*

In late 1994, after a decade of experience in the physical world of brand design, I slipped into cyberspace, in part inspired by Jeff Bezos' launch of Amazon. I plunged headlong into the emerging Web industry with Resource Marketing—now called Ten/Resource—a pioneering technology marketing company of which I became president in 2001. In this new adventure in new media I was able to spread my virtual wings, applying my understanding of the consumer, brands, and customer experience to the interactive marketing needs of companies such as Apple, CompuServe (now part of AOL), Burton Snowboards, CondéNet, and Victoria's Secret.

From 1997 through 2000, as the strategy director at Resource, I spent thousands of hours assessing the total customer experience on e-commerce sites as seen from the consumer perspective. This involved over 1000 purchases and returns and thousands of customer service interactions. The resulting Resource eCommerce Watch™ research reports were hailed as the first comprehensive, consumer-centric studies of the end-to-end e-retail experience.

I was intent on understanding how expectations from the physical space carry over to the digital world. And I wanted to define what it takes to make a great total customer experience online.

These findings and insights boiled down to a simple thought: The Web gives us greater control than ever before. More control means more power. And more power means increasing demands.

PREFACE

And because, while we may surf the Web, we live in the real world, those demands spill over into every interaction we have with a merchant, company, or organization, online or off.

Companies need a roadmap for this new landscape, one that provides them with direction for improving the quality and the consistency of every customer interaction, no matter the locale or the category. So, I present to you a framework for thinking about consumer needs and demands, and for changing your channels into fluid streams of experience that meet those demands wherever they exist.

The Ten Demandments are simple guidelines to be shared across departments and between layers, not hoarded by, or herded into, a single silo. So take these Demandments, learn them, and live them. They are the guides to turning even your most demanding consumers into your most delighted customers.

But my learning process never ends. I'm interested in your ideas, your stories, and your *demands.* I invite you to share them with me.

Kelly Mooney
kmooney10@columbus.rr.com
Ten Worldwide
343 North Front Street
Columbus, OH 43215
www.tendemandments.com

introduction

BEFORE YOU BEGIN reading this book, ask yourself this question: Are you worthy of the loyalty you desire?

If the honest answer is "Yes!"—congratulations! Yours is one of the few companies that actually understands what your consumers really want. But if the answer—the *honest* answer—is anything less than an emphatic affirmative, then ask yourself why. Or rather, why not?

The answer probably is right in front of your face. So go look in the mirror. What do you see? A consumer, that's what. You may be many things—a professional, a partner, a parent—but no matter what else you are, you're also a consumer. We all are.

And that, in a way, is what this book is about. *The Ten Demandments* examines the universal truths about what today's consumers want, need, and demand. Then it puts them in the perspective of today's challenges and changes, from advances in technology to specialization of products, relationship management to niche marketing. And it expresses these issues as seen from the perspective of consumers as well as executives who have tackled many of these same challenges.

While consumer demands may vary widely from category to category, channel to channel, brand to brand, and life-stage to life-stage, when you look down from the mountaintop at our common experiences, you realize that heightened expectations for honesty, control, guidance, quality, and service apply to every consumer, and every company, everywhere. You demand no less of the companies you give your business to than your consumers demand of your company. And they deserve no less, too.

This book is not about generic experiences or expectations, but rather about universal ones. That's why it examines the holistic needs of consumers and applies them to our changing world in specific, actionable ways. It explores how consumers' lives are changing, and how companies can evolve to anticipate new consumer demands. And it discusses the need for companies to keep clearing a bar that's being perpetually raised by competition, innovation, and experiences that delight and attract consumers in new and interesting ways.

Staying ahead of that ever-widening curve of change in the marketplace is your greatest challenge. And this book lays down the law according to consumers about what they want, expect, and demand from you now, as they stand on the outer limits of that curve.

WELCOME TO THE AGE OF THE DEMANDING CONSUMER

Ask anyone who hates one brand but loves another why they feel that way. Probably the answer is that one brand does nothing for them, and the other does everything for them. That's a big difference. Which side of that fence does your company fall on most often?

Talk to almost any executive and you'll find they're all in agreement about one emerging truth: Today's consumers expect more and tolerate less. And while consumers have been treated to any number of changes that have expanded their options and enriched their experiences—from mega-malls to personal shoppers, niche products to satellite TV—one innovation in the past decade rises above all others for having wrought the most dramatic change in consumer exposure to empowering experiences, range of options, and breadth of resources: the Internet.

Thanks to the Internet, consumers can compare prices and features in a few seconds, study up on illnesses before they contract them, exchange photos moments after taking them, order the perfect outfit for tomorrow night's party, and dash off an email to any company on the planet, fully anticipating a reply.

Computers and the Internet have become so persistent and embedded in modern life that they're now commonplace tools in our everyday arsenal of devices for communication and information. Like the telephone, television, and radio (and telegraph and printing press, if you want to go way back), the Internet connects people with each other and companies with their consumers, in ground-breaking, barrier-shattering ways.

As we've become more confident and competent in its use, the Web has made us more confident and competent as consumers, and therefore more demanding in researching, negotiating, and buying everything. Everywhere. And that's both a challenge and an opportunity.

This book is *not* about the Internet, but rather about what, in part, the Internet hath wrought, in terms of consumer expectations and demands, and the ways that companies must strive to meet these increased needs in every channel and with every interaction.

Long-term relationships are the brass ring for companies that hope to grow and prosper over time; and those relationships begin and end at the many touch-points where consumers and companies come together. Consumers that interact in every channel are the most loyal, the most profitable, and the most vital to any organization.

These interactions, whether good or bad, inspiring or frustrating, define the relationship consumers have with a brand. Or whether they will even have a relationship with a brand. No matter where your consumers connect with your company—in stores, through product use, via packaging, advertising, marketing, direct mail, PR, toll-free numbers, email, Web sites, or through personal interactions—these points of contact need to be both integrated and consistent across the continuum of, and for, your overall brand.

Consumers are already overloaded with too many variations on the same themes, already confused by unaligned channels or misguided marketing attempts, so the last thing they need is to have to figure out why they can't return a dress at your store just because they bought it at your dot.com instead. It's all the same company, right? A brand is a brand is a brand. That's how they see you, whether or not that's how you operate.

No matter how many organizational layers you've got to peel back or which silos you have to tear down, your company must now find a way to thread all your touch points through the eye of the needle, which represents the eye of the beholder. It's a narrow passageway to be sure, with little room for error, but all your points of contact, your brand messages, your interactions and your communications must converge and support each other as they pass through the portal of the consumer experience. Consumers must have one view of your company and your brand, no matter how many uncoordinated efforts or warring factions may lurk behind the scenes.

Rebecca Kotch, Vice President of Retail for House of Blues, says that the Web serves as "a thread woven throughout the whole company. It really ties the company together, particularly because we have the club business and the concert business. So [our Web site] shows the House of Blues relationship with the artist. It reaffirms that we support music and that we promote new artists," she says. "You know, really, everything comes off of that spine."

As consumers become increasingly aware of seamless and compelling experiences like those offered by House of Blues, they will also take greater notice of companies that lack tangible integration or fail to serve up a cohesive, meaningful brand experience. Thus, companies must aggressively pursue internal alignment to meet these consumer demands, or face the consequences of slower growth and lost loyalty.

This book will not help you identify *who* your consumers are, but it will help you think more deeply about *how* they want to be treated throughout the total consumer experience. *The Ten Demandments* provides a lens through which you can view your world, your company, and your brand as seen through the eyes of your consumers. And it will challenge your company to ask and answer five key questions vital to your future success:

1. Does our company know how our consumers *really* feel about us?
2. Does our executive leadership advocate a customer religion?
3. Does every associate understand his or her role in delivering a total customer experience that's unified, integrated, and consumer-centric?
4. Do we have key metrics that measure and reward consumer satisfaction and loyalty?
5. Are we worthy of consumer loyalty?

Delivering a great total customer experience, in its most simplistic form, is about cultivating relationships. And the job of cultivating relationships cannot be relegated solely to the front lines, to the customer service department, to the CRM team, or to the marketing group. It's everyone's job and everybody's duty.

But the inspiration must come from the top, from leaders who mandate, champion, and evangelize a consumer-centric philosophy, vision, and long-term direction. Once expressed, this philosophy must permeate every part of the organization. Every initiative. Every measurement. Every new idea. Every investment, from technology to infrastructure, from research and development to human resources and holiday hires. This philosophy must unify your organization as if it were a rallying cry, a reason for being, and a higher calling. Because in the end you're in business for one purpose: to provide products or services to your consumers. And if they're not buying, then you're not selling. End of story.

If we've learned anything over the last few years as the Internet bubble stretched to the breaking point and then burst with a calamitous bang, it's that technology is not the answer. But it is an enabler, delivering experiences and organizing information in ways that have rocked the world. Still, it can just as easily enable a bad experience as a good one, and deliver to consumers exactly what they don't need, don't want, and don't care about.

If asked directly, most people within a company could tell you what would make their consumers more satisfied. Yet they don't act upon that knowledge because they don't see it as their job. Day in, day out, they're directed—and measured—by a different set of criteria, ones that often map back to short-term management initiatives or operational efficiencies instead of strategic goals directed at winning greater consumer loyalty.

For example, many contact centers still train representatives to hang up the telephone within two minutes of taking a call, and measure (and reward) their success on their ability to do so, regardless of whether the customer's issue was adequately handled in that time. The calls may be short, but they aren't often sweet.

On the other hand, companies such as Hewlett-Packard, which are devoted to serving their consumers' real needs rather than to reducing their call times, are using open-ended closure techniques that are designed to satisfy and resolve customer issues and to ensure that each customer leaves the interaction with a positive feeling about the company. This up-front investment of time can yield a long-term benefit in customer loyalty. And because a customer's problem often is resolved with the first call, he may not need to call back again and again for more help, saving time and money down the line. So in the end these tactics not only make for happier customers, they foster less time-consuming and more trusting relationships as well.

"You need the manager of the manager of the manager to understand that it may be cheaper to have that support open-ended and have the agents do what it takes to satisfy the customer," explains Alex Sozonoff, Vice President, Customer Advocacy for Hewlett-Packard.

It's not that today's consumers are so much more demanding than those of other eras, it's just that their demands have been pent up owing to the lack of any better experience. Like the mythical Pandora's Box, the Web browser, once opened, can never truly be closed again. And consumers, having tasted the power, control, and variety offered by the online experience, are unwilling to settle for anything less, no matter where they interact with a brand or a company. But consumers are not unreasonable: Meeting (better yet, exceeding) their initial expectations can help companies head off far more costly demands down the line.

This book uses many well-known brands, as well as some lesser known ones, as examples, but the insights here can help any company or organization whose survival is dependent upon deeper, more meaningful relationships. Whether you sell products or services to consumers or serve the public good through public services such as government or education, the universal truths of the Ten Demandments still apply.

You'll notice that there's no single case study saluting one company that exceptionally fulfills all of these Demandments; that's because although most companies meet some of them, none seems to meet absolutely all of them with equal finesse. At least, not yet. And that's quite all right.

It's not imperative that your company embrace each of the Demandments fully and completely to succeed in meeting your consumers' needs. Some of the Ten Demandments will apply more to your company than will others, depending upon your category, your consumer base, and your business objectives. Every company has different priorities and needs, as does every consumer.

But it is important that you tackle the ones that resonate most with your consumers, based on what you know about them, your business, and your competition. To survive and thrive in this highly competitive landscape where consumer demands can make or break you, your company must strive to excel—really excel—in at least three of the Ten Demandments that mean the most to your consumers. If you can't do that, ultimately you will fail.

But if you honor the voice of today's consumers by listening and learning, reacting and responding, to their needs and demands, you will not only succeed now, you will flourish in the future.

THE TEN DEMANDMENTS IN A NUTSHELL

1. **Earn my trust . . .** This is about respect, integrity, advocacy, and quality. Forget all the others if you can't master this one.
2. **Inspire me . . .** Craft meaningful emotional connections with your consumers through immersive experiences, motivating messages, and relevant philanthropy. Inspirational brands that transcend their own products and services, become greater than the sum of their parts.

3. **Make it easy** . . . Simplicity, speed, and usefulness are the keys to consumer ease. Don't confuse complexity with progress. The best things in life are often the easiest.

4. **Put me in charge** . . . Consumers expect choices and control, particularly from service organizations that can enable self-paced self-service. Put consumers in the driver's seat or they'll peel out of your parking lot without a second thought.

5. **Guide me** . . . Too much white noise, too little context—that's the problem. So filter the chaos with expert advice, education, and information. And stand shoulder-to-shoulder with your consumers as they move through the decision-making process and beyond.

6. **24/7** . . . Anytime, anywhere access . . . that's the ticket in this 'round the clock world. Nine-to-five hours won't cut it for consumers who expect companies to be there for them all the time, no matter the channel.

7. **Get to know me** . . . You can't win consumer loyalty without understanding what consumers want. Listen, learn, and study up on their real lives, don't just dive into the data pool.

8. **Exceed my expectations** . . . Even demanding consumers can be wowed, so woo them by overdelivering through uncommon courtesies, surprising services, and go-the-extra-mile efforts that show you really care.

9. **Reward me** . . . Treat your consumers like the VIPs they are to you. Acknowledge and build their loyalty by rewarding them with points programs, privileged access, or other winning ways.

10. **Stay with me** . . . Relationships are built not in a day, but in a lifetime, so stay with your consumers if you want

them to stay with you. Deliver on postpurchase promises, stay in touch in meaningful ways, and evolve your brand to meet your consumers' evolving needs over time.

01

The First
Demandment

earn my trust

ONCE UPON A TIME there was a land where sales clerks knew their customers by name, where people shopped at the same local stores for decades, and where parents were amused when their tots hummed commercial jingles from Saturday morning TV. The consumer path to loyalty for brands was straightforward: If you knew your consumers, showed them good faith, provided them with great service, and offered them quality products, you would win their hearts and wallets. As their loyalty grew, they spread that brand dedication by word of mouth to other consumers. And everyone lived happily ever after.

End of story. That fairytale may still exist in some hidden corners of the world, but most brands must now battle for consumer trust and loyalty amid a changing landscape of myriad competitors and varieties, multichannel commerce, big-box stores, and consumer cynicism the likes of which has never been seen before. The mix is even more volatile because of the dangerous times in which we live—with threats both physical and digital to our privacy, security, and information, we feel at risk even at home, and are far less willing to trust without verification.

Living in a time of too many stores, too many brands, and too many choices, the companies that have stood the test of time and served several generations have a strong head start in maintaining and extending consumer loyalty. In surveys conducted by organizations such as the Harris Poll, consumers have frequently ranked Johnson & Johnson, makers of Johnson's Baby Shampoo (among many other products), at or near the top of the list of brands they most trust. Any brand that gets millions of consumers to entrust their babies to its products is clearly onto a good thing.

THE VOICE OF THE CUSTOMER
PLAY FAIR.

> This can't be you against me. If I can't trust you, nothing else you do even matters. I need to trust that you're not out to gouge me with high prices or underperforming, overpromising products. I expect good value for my money. Reassure me that your products will deliver and that I'm getting a good deal. I expect to get what I pay for, so don't let me down and I won't let you down.

Longevity and long-standing, daily presence in consumer homes certainly helps build trust and ward off recent competitors. In the news media that's a particularly important quality, with newspapers forced to compete against not only their print rivals but also network and cable news, the Internet, radio, and wireless news feeds. With so many media-company mergers, many organizations (including AOL/Time Warner, which also owns CNN) are consolidating their reporting and redistributing it through multiple-branded delivery channels. This can make it hard for relatively lone wolves like the stalwart *New York Times* to maintain eminence.

But after 150 years in print, "the Old Gray Lady," as the *Times* is often known, has managed to keep its ink in the black and its readership in the millions. Why? Because the strength of its brand is legendary and trustworthy, having become as much an American institution as it is a media brand. Yet it evolved with the times, launching into cyberspace with emailed headline news and a content-rich Web site that keeps its readers in touch even when the hard-copy paper is out of reach.

Living up to its reputation as a source of reliable and quality information, the paper's Web site, which requires (free) one-time registration to access, provides a lengthy and complete policy disclosure that explains how online reader behavior is tracked, measured, and used, including even how its banner advertising is targeted to viewers. The Old Gray Lady may be an institution, but she's still pretty spry—and tech-savvy—for her age.

THE VOICE OF THE CUSTOMER
LOSE THE FINE PRINT.

Who hasn't seen a car commercial that flashes the sales conditions on screen for a second—usually in tiny type—as if anyone could read the fine print in that amount of time? Or who has had to click through a maze of pages on a Web site

> just to find a customer-care phone number or return policy? I
> can't stand it when a company buries the truth in a set of dis-
> claimers that only a bloodhound could find. Get your info to
> me upfront, and in large print, so I know I can trust you.

Companies can no longer be in the business of merely selling to
consumers, or resting on their laurels of longevity; they must radi-
cally shift their own philosophy and methods so that they are always
serving consumers, and serving them well. Service, quality, and
value are so intricately intertwined with consumer trust and loyalty
that if a company fails to deliver on any of those three key criteria,
they can kiss their customers good-bye. Period.

That's why the First Demandment—**Earn My Trust**—is also the
most important. Trust comes first in this rulebook, in large part because it's at the heart of the new consumer experience, as well as
having been the centerpiece of the old-fashioned consumer experience. No matter where a buyer interacts with a brand—in a store, at
a service center, online, or on the phone—trust is a fluid commodity that ebbs and flows with each experience.

**TRUST IS A FLUID COMMODITY
THAT EBBS AND FLOWS
WITH EACH EXPERIENCE.**

The lessons of this First
Demandment are clear-cut:
Online or off, by phone or
mail, or face to face, consumers demand a high level of respect, service, and quality from the companies to which they give their business. If they're already familiar with a brand and have grown to trust
it, they expect that their loyalty has not been misplaced. If they're
entering into a new relationship with a company, they are cautiously
optimistic that their trust will not be abused. But they may lose
faith in a brand that does them wrong, no matter how long-standing the relationship, thinking a company that has failed them once
will probably do it again if given the opportunity.

A TITLE WAVE

The titles cropping up in executive teams are often the first signs of a wave of change sweeping through the corporate world. In the 1980s the Chief Marketing Officer (CMO) was suddenly in vogue, and marketing and branding ascended to new heights of importance as businesses sought to capture a swiftly moving audience.

With the advent of the Internet the titles sprouted like wildflowers, from the silly charm of the Chief Yahoos! (the founders of Yahoo!) to the aesthetic appeal of Chief Experience Officers (CXO), whose role involved defining and championing the customer experience.

Now, new titles are catching on that have a decidedly customer-centric focus. The Chief Customer Officer (CCO) has a title that pretty much says it all—supporting the customer's point of view within the walls of the company. Other variations on this CXO or CCO title include Chief Consumer Advocate (CCA) and Consumer Satisfaction Officer (CSO). No matter the initials, the job is basically to ensure that the ideals of customer service and consumer satisfaction are championed within an organization.

Likewise, it's no coincidence that Chief Privacy Officers (CPOs) are suddenly appearing on executive teams at Fortune 500 companies like Microsoft, IBM, and AT&T. It's an important role at companies struggling with the moral, ethical, and marketing dilemmas associated with CRM technologies and issues.

By serving as the in-house policy chief for consumer privacy and protection, the CPO sets the agenda for company standards and infuses and enforces them throughout the organization. Taking the high road by promoting and protecting consumers' best interests within a company is a smart move at every turn. And no matter the title, it's a job that must be done.

There's no question that dedicating executive-level positions to consumer concerns and/or privacy issues is a smart move . . . or is there? Not everyone thinks that such roles are necessary. "I wouldn't suggest we would need a Chief Customer Officer, Customer Service Officer, [or] Consumer Officer . . . absolutely not," says Paul Charron, CEO of Liz Claiborne. "Every general manager has got to be focused on the consumer. Obviously, as the seniormost executive in the company, I should be the most focused on the consumer."

But sometimes, says Alex Sozonoff, Vice President of Customer Advocacy for Hewlett-Packard, a large organization needs a dedicated executive to rally the troops and help re-align priorities across units. "In other words," he says, you need someone to pull "the silos together and create one face to the customer." Sozonoff, who reports directly to CEO Carly Fiorina, serves as the voice of the customer within the expansive HP organization. "I would put meetings together and say, 'Well, this is not a customer view. You should be looking at it from the outside in rather than from the inside out.'" Sozonoff believes that having dedicated internal advocates for the customer point of view is helping HP to become a more "customer-centric kind of company."

Years of good faith based on pleasant in-store experiences can be erased in a few clicks if a consumer gets a virtual slap in the face at that same brand's e-commerce site. In fact, according to Jupiter

Media Metrix, Inc., 70 percent of online shoppers said that poor online customer service from a multichannel retailer could lead them to spend less at the site's brick-and-mortar store counterpart.

Similar trust-busters can take place in any number of touchpoints and areas of sensitivity, from violating a consumer's sense of privacy by selling or bartering their personal information without permission (or obtaining it through misleading policies) to producing, marketing, or falsely advertising lousy products or unreliable services. Bottom line: A bad experience is often more memorable than a good one, and consumers tend to remember when they've been treated wrong more often than when they've been treated right.

THE VOICE OF THE CUSTOMER
STRAIGHT TALK, NOT SLICK TALK.

A little double-speak goes a long way, so cut it out altogether. Your policies and communications should tell me what I need to know right off the bat. I hate having to second-guess what you mean. That's what I love about the Land's End guarantee: "Guaranteed. Period." Simple and to the point. Get it?

Here's how to straighten up . . .

- **Stop pretending.** Lots of companies present themselves as Jacks of all trades, but then come across as masters of none. It's hard to tell exactly what they really do, much less what they do really well. So don't try to act like you can do it all just to land my business. Be clear and direct about your strengths, and I'll stop to listen.

- **If you say something, mean it**. Don't send me mixed messages, bait-and-switch me with promotions for out-of-stock stuff, or tell me one thing in your ads and then try to change the story when I'm in your store or on your site. The brands I like best do what they do best everywhere I see them. They keep their promises, and don't pull any punches.

- **Honesty is the best policy**. I don't want to go through your dirty laundry, but I do expect you to be honest with me. Get out the news quickly about changes at your company, info on your products, and problems you may be having. Use your site to share press releases and statements about what you've been up to; even if you've been in the news for all the wrong reasons, I'd like to hear your side of the story (if it's honestly told).

A BAD EXPERIENCE IN ONE CHANNEL CAN SMEAR THE BRAND IN ALL ITS CHANNELS. While the standards of channel loyalty still seem to hold true for most consumers, with all the options before them now they're more likely to experiment in other channels of a brand they like. And a bad experience in one channel can smear the brand and all its channels, just as a good experience will burnish the brand's image across all channels. Thus, while consumers may frequent one channel over another, their trust, and therefore brand loyalty, is now built *across* channels, not *within* them.

Every channel and touch point is a new opportunity to build a relationship with customers, but it also offers a new way to fail them, so companies must be ever-vigilant about managing their experiences everywhere, in every way.

* PROGRESSIVE THINKING

While comparison shopping has long been a part of the consumer psyche, companies are beginning to realize the value of helping shoppers find the best deals. Progressive Insurance was the first (and remains the only) auto insurance company to roll out this method of building consumers' trust by steering them toward the best insurance buy for their needs, even if it's not from Progressive.

Progressive has been in business since 1937, and it had gained a reputation, in large part, of being a high-risk insurer, offering insurance to drivers who had a few black marks on their record. But in 1988, after a California initiative was passed that came down hard on the insurance industry for noncompetitive practices, then-CEO (and son of one of the company's founders) Peter Lewis started down a path that led the company in a new direction—he called his old college friend, Ralph Nader, who was supporting the California initiative. Lewis asked Nader what was so wrong with the insurance industry. Nader said that it was difficult for consumers to compare prices or shop around for insurance from different companies. Lewis thought his friend was mistaken, but after further research he realized that Nader was on to something. And a price-comparison powerhouse was born.

According to Alan Bauer, Business Leader at Progressive, the company first provided price-comparison services to customers for a fee, then abandoned that model and instead offered it as a free service to potential customers via the telephone direct-sales channel. Consumer reaction was so positive that Progressive realized it might have a marketable point of differentiation on its hands.

"Once we incorporated [the price comparison service] into our marketing message, I think people really got a different feel about what Progressive was," Bauer recalls. "It was pretty clear that this was a powerful way to make the phone ring."

Progressive has built a strong foundation on the basis of this "Aha!" insight—that consumers really wanted to compare prices among various insurance providers, and that the company could build consumer trust and loyalty by helping people shop around for insurance.

Having leaped from its 1980 ranking of 43rd place among major U.S. private passenger auto insurers to a startling 9th place, nationwide, in 1993, and now to a 4th-place position, Progressive is clearly on a roll with its consumer-centric focus.

"The phrase 'consumer experience' is something that's on our lips more and more," Bauer says, adding "we want everyone to know that we are the best auto insurer in the history of auto insurance. And that's what we're going to focus on. So, more and more, you're going to see us polishing what we offer consumers, making it more accessible, more interesting, and loved by them."

It doesn't help that brands must overcome bad experiences inflicted on consumers by competitors (how many nice car salesmen have been sullied by the tactics of their less-ethical peers?); but that guilt by association can be turned to a company's advantage by taking the high road and upping the ante, creating and evangelizing for the best possible and most consistently high-quality experiences across all their brand channels. Set higher standards for your own company, as Progressive did, if your industry is notoriously unresponsive to consumers' needs, and you'll reap the rewards of increased consumer trust while also forcing your competitors to play catch-up.

With so many opportunities for failure or success at every consumer touch point, brand strength is a revolving door that opens and closes on multiple channels at each turn. That's the 360-degree brand experience. It revolves, and evolves, every day. And only through holistic, consumer-centered experiences will brands be able to survive and thrive in this circular, and often cyclical, marketplace.

✳ THE VOICE OF THE CUSTOMER
PROVE YOU'RE ON MY SIDE.

Prove you're willing and able to act on my behalf, even if it means losing the short-term sale or limiting how much leeway you have with my personal information. Be my advocate and I'll take notice.

Here are a few hints for being on my side . . .

- **Suggest a competitor.** When you don't have what I need, tell me someone who might. Or go a step further, the way Progressive Insurance does—help me that find the best deal, even if it's not from you. When you show me that you're looking out for my interests, regardless of whether you get the sale, I'm likely to turn to you the next time.

- **Respect me and my data.** Show me you care by telling me, in detail, about what you'll be doing with any information I share with you. Spell out, in easy-to-find privacy and security policies, how my information will be used. If you have plans to share or sell my information, get my permission first. If you change your policies let me know, and give me an easy way out if I no longer agree with them.

- **Share the wealth.** When I share my personal information with you, I expect to get something meaningful in return—whether it's a more personalized experience, better prices, or special offers geared toward my interests. And if you're cashing in on my personal information—with my consent, of course—cut me in on the deal by giving me reward points or something else of value. That way we both benefit.

BRAND STRENGTH IS A REVOLVING DOOR THAT OPENS AND CLOSES ON MULTIPLE CHANNELS AT EACH TURN.

Nothing invokes consumer anxiety as palpably as being confronted by a screen full of personal questions on a Web site registration page, pages of blanks to be filled in on an application form, or the third degree coming over the phone line from an unseen customer service representative or telemarketer. What information you ask for, and how, when, and why you ask for it, are all critical elements in whether consumers will feel comfortable sharing their personal details. Irrelevant, repetitive, inappropriate, or downright suspect questions raise more than an eyebrow these days—they can raise genuine fears among consumers that their information, once released, could fall into the hands of identity-thieves or other data evil-doers.

Look no farther than the hilariously thought-provoking television commercial for Internet service provider (ISP) EarthLink that began airing in the fall of 2001. It shows a woman and man in a bar, getting to know each other. The man asks for the woman's phone number and she gives it to him. Then, while the woman is still sitting there, both the bartender and another patron ask the man if they can have her phone number, too—and he offers to sell it to them for $5 each, much to the horror of the woman who had just entrusted him with her number. It's an amusingly chilling portrayal of what can happen when a consumer willingly gives out personal contact or other information, only to have it transferred—and often sold!—to other companies with whom they hadn't intended to share their info.

But consumer concerns about what happens to their information when it leaves their possession are only part of the equation in the trust factor—consumers also need to be convinced that the value of the information they provide will be matched by an equal or greater return on this information investment in the form of a better experience, more customized service, or other positive benefit that maps back to their needs.

Today's consumers seek a new kind of ROI that delivers a return on the information they have shared with a company, knowing full well that their data is a commodity that may be shared, bought, or sold. So when a company starts out by asking too many questions too soon, or getting too cozy too fast without delivering on the promise of a markedly improved experience, it endangers those first tenuous tendrils of trust that sprout between companies and consumers during the early stages of their relationship.

Companies have to ensure that their consumers also feel safe giving them information, doing that by protecting their data from prying eyes and hacking hands. Consumers—especially those who shop or bank online—are becoming increasingly aware of the dangers of fraud associated with lax security for their personal or financial information. According to the Pew Internet & American Life

Project, 86 percent of Internet users have expressed some concern about online privacy.

When major celebrities like Oprah Winfrey or Steven Spielberg become targets of identity thieves—as happened when a New York City busboy did some digital digging and came up with their credit card information and other pertinent financial data—people begin to realize just how vulnerable their own, less-protected information is to those digging for data pay dirt.

And when even the reporters who cover issues of security and protection are easy targets of fraud—as happened when several investigative journalists attending a conference in Chicago during the summer of 2001 had their credit card numbers stolen and used for online purchases—consumers rightfully begin to wonder if even taking careful measures will really protect them.

> LOSS OF CONTROL OVER THE FUNDAMENTAL FACTS AND FIGURES OF THEIR LIVES RIGHTFULLY SCARES PEOPLE.

Over time, as consumer awareness of data-security dangers grows, every credit card transaction, application form, or customer survey they face will seem suspect if they don't know how that information will be used, what other data it will be cross-referenced with, or who will eventually have access to it. This loss of control over the fundamental facts and figures of their lives rightfully scares people, and heightens their suspicions about who's doing the asking, and why.

✳ THE VOICE OF THE CUSTOMER
DON'T BE PUSHY.

Don't pounce on me when I first meet you, or force me to tell you everything about me before I know anything about you.

That's like going on a one-sided blind date. And go easy on the questions. Everywhere I turn, people want to know way too much about me. Does RadioShack really need to know my ZIP code before it can sell me a battery? Give me a break! When you start asking questions, make sure they're relevant to what I'm buying. It's fine to greet me at the door with a friendly "Hello," but don't try to sell me anything right off the bat, or bug me if I'm just browsing.

As Harrison "Lee" Rainie, Director of the Pew Internet & American Life Project, testified before a congressional subcommittee hearing on privacy issues in May 2001, "'Privacy' means several things to Americans. For some it means anonymity, for others it means confidentiality (that information will not be disclosed to others), and for others it means security (that malicious outsiders cannot get at the information)."

Still, there's a funny contradiction in how consumers feel about their privacy, and the steps they take to protect it. While research has shown that people put more faith and trust in companies that wear their privacy policies on their sleeves (by, say, prominently posting them on sites, distributing them at service counters, and sending them out in the mail), it turns out that the fine print of privacy protection policies overwhelms many consumers, deterring them from digging into critical details of disclosure.

During the spring and summer of 2001, Americans were deluged with privacy statements from financial services institutions (as required by the Gramm-Leach-Bliley Act of 2000). Yet only about 1 percent of consumers actually read the policies that spell out how and where their information was being used or shared. Most recipients simply chucked the statements into the trash, or filed them away without even a cursory glance. And very few consumers chose to opt out of having their information shared or sold, despite the fact that every privacy policy was required to offer directions on how to do so.

Not surprisingly, many of the unread policies—which frequently resembled the flimsy statements about rule changes inserted into credit card or bank statements—were written in language and displayed in a type size that only a lawyer could love. While companies had many months to send out these alerts before the July 1, 2001, deadline, many complied only at the last minute.

The result: Consumers were suddenly swamped with so many privacy mailings that they paid little attention to *any* of them. Whether or not this was the desired intention of the companies, the timing and nature of their mailings were almost guaranteed to overwhelm their customers into ignoring these critical communications.

In contrast, companies, such as American Express, that sent out their policies earlier that spring often provided meaningful educational statements that served to inform their customers and strengthen their trust.

Protecting consumer information here and now is only part of the story, though. Companies must start thinking ahead to where and how they'll be using, and thus protecting, consumer information down the road. The advent of interactive television systems such as TiVo, for instance, spawned a firestorm of outrage among consumer advocacy groups when it became clear that interactive TV is capable of essentially watching the watchers through technology that can track, monitor, collect, and react to consumer viewing habits and interests in ways that go far beyond the old-fangled Nielsen rating system.

✳ FULL DISCLOSURE: DON'T LEAVE HOME WITHOUT IT

American Express has long set the standard for financial institutions when informing customers about policies and privileges. In keeping with this heritage, it was one of the first major institutions to send out a comprehensive and easy-to-understand privacy policy in compliance with the requirements of the Gramm-Leach-Bliley Act of 2000.

In early 2001, the company sent cardholders a comprehensive but readable notice explaining exactly how it protects their privacy when it collects and uses their information.

The law also requires that companies tell consumers how to opt out of having their information shared, and AmEx gave its customers a variety of ways to do so, including a toll-free number, a postage-paid response card, and an online form.

These easy and actionable opt-out methods clearly back up the opening sentence in the privacy notice mailing: "At American Express, maintaining our customers' trust and confidence is a high priority." Now that's customer service.

Television that tunes in to its viewers' habits is a scary idea to many people—and it's only the proverbial tip of the technological iceberg, as new and improved devices push information and track user activities and movements. Consumers are just now waking up to the fact that their cool toys, from PDAs to GPS units, are capable of recording and reporting on their behavior to the outside world.

And yet the harsh reality of our post-September 11th era is that people are also waking up to the likelihood of government surveillance and electronic monitoring for national security purposes. In recent years, when the words *privacy* and *security* were spoken in the same sentence on Capitol Hill, they were usually linked as mutually dependent ideas related to respecting and protecting consumer information in the new world of widespread data dissemination. Congress has held numerous hearings about consumer privacy issues, and the federal government has set strict standards around issues such as collecting information from children.

But since September 11, 2001, Americans have been told that people may have to give up some of their civil liberties, including certain privacy rights, for the greater good of national security. No doubt Uncle Sam will keep an eye on how consumer information is collected and used, but he's got bigger fish to fry for the foreseeable future. In October 2001, the Federal Trade Commission (FTC), which had been driving many of the efforts to delve deeper into privacy protections, announced that it would not be focusing its efforts on new consumer protection laws, but would instead concentrate on stronger enforcement of existing laws.

> SMART COMPANIES WILL GO THE EXTRA MILE TO WRAP THEIR CONSUMERS IN A WARM BLANKET OF PROTECTION.

The public tolerance for privacy invasions may increase as a result of the war against terrorism. But the smart companies will go the extra mile to wrap their consumers in a warm blanket of protection through improved electronic security and closer scrutiny of business partners and practices, to prevent abuse of consumer information.

It's a dangerous world out there, and consumers are looking to established institutions—including major companies—for reassurance and a sense of well-being. So today's brands must relate to their consumers in multiple ways—winning consumers' initial trust through ethical behavior, open communications, and discretion in collecting and using information; preserving and strengthening established bonds through ongoing thoughtful and respectful consumer care; and staying ahead of the curve of the growing range of technological and ethical dilemmas on the horizon.

From the increasing risk of identity theft to the rising popularity of membership loyalty programs, every opportunity to grow consumer

EVERY OPPORTUNITY TO GROW CONSUMER TRUST IS ALSO PLANTED WITH THE SEEDS OF BRAND DESTRUCTION.

trust is also planted with the seeds of brand destruction. Tending to this fragile garden requires constant care for and concern about the protection of consumers, their information, and their good faith.

THE VOICE OF THE CUSTOMER
PROTECT ME.

> I've always expected that you'd keep me safe from physical harm when I'm in your location or using your products. Now I expect that you'll keep me safe from digital harm as well. So work hard to keep my information safe and secure. And alert me if there's been a security breach, so I at least have fair warning that someone may be about to charge up all my credit cards. IKEA sent me an email when their online catalog sign-up list was compromised; no harm was done, but it really made me feel good that they had alerted me just the same.

Today's consumers are far less willing to forgive, and far more likely to take offense than those who came before them. They have more choices than ever before, and while that can be overwhelming, it can also be empowering. When your brand of toothpaste is only one among many, you've got to work that much harder to prove your value to a consumer who may switch brands on a whim if not embraced in a loyal relationship.

Established trust is a brand's to lose. Long-trusted brands wear a patina of authority and integrity that consumers will automatically respect unless given a reason to feel otherwise. Both Ford and Firestone stumbled badly during the 2000 scandal over faulty—and ultimately, fatal—tires on Ford vehicles. But Firestone came out the worse for the wear, as the primary manufacturer and the slower responder of the two companies to the public outcry. While Ford also had wounds to lick, its strong statements of public apology and renewed commitment to quality have helped it get back on the road, if slowly.

The lessons to be learned from the real and virtual worlds are equally compelling, and equally critical to earning and keeping consumer trust. No matter where or how you touch the lives of consumers, you won't get very far if you break the implicit faith they show in your company each time they hand over their money, information, or commitment.

Consumers haven't lost control at that point—they've actually seized it, because they still own their trust, and it's theirs to keep and yours to lose. You've got to deliver on your promises, play fair, and show some respect, or you can count yourself out of the running. Without trust, nothing else matters. With trust, anything is possible.

DEMANDMENT 01: **EARN MY TRUST—SELF-EVALUATION**

Now that you've read this Demandment, see how you stack up. The checkpoints in this form reflect the key takeaways from the "Voice of the Customer" sections. Identify where your company could stand some improvement, and you'll have a shot at building bridges with the people who keep you in business.

1. EARN MY TRUST	Excellent	Good	Poor
Play fair.	Prices reflect good value and are competitive across the board.	Prices are competitive on most products.	Prices are not competitive.
Lose the fine print.	Key info and sales conditions are prominently and explicitly communicated.	Key info and sales conditions are explicitly communicated.	Key info and sales conditions are intentionally buried.
Straight talk, not slick talk.	Clear, honest claims and communications are business as usual.	Honest claims and communications.	Claimed and communications lack clarity and honesty.
Prove you're on my side.	Policies reflect a philosophy of customer advocacy, even if it means losing a sale.	Policies reflect a philosophy of customer advocacy but execution is inconsistent.	Polices do not reflect a philosophy of customer advocacy.
Don't be pushy.	Questions are optional, relevant, and allow consumers to answer them at their own pace.	Consumers answer questions at their own pace.	Consumers are requested to answer questions prior to a transaction or brand experience.
Protect me.	Employ a Chief Privacy Officer or equivalent to ensure consumer privacy and security protection.	Employ a consumer advocate to ensure privacy and security protection, but not at an executive level.	It's nobody's primary job to advocate for consumer privacy and security protection.

02

The Second Demandment

inspire me

IT'S THE SPARK THAT LIGHTS A FLAME, the adrenaline rush of a breakthrough when anything is possible, the inexplicable rapture of unexpected joy. That's the power of inspiration: the impact of emotional and exhilarating connectivity that speaks to the soul, the heart, and the mind in both a whisper and a shout.

In a world where brand survival depends on crafting an emotional bond with consumers, the companies that plumb the depths at which the products, service, experiences, or ideals resonate with their customers are the ones that will thrive over time.

Connecting with consumers in meaningful, long-lasting ways isn't easy. Sure, you can get folks to cry at TV spots featuring newborn babies or blushing brides, and you can get kids hyped up over the latest action figure from a hit cartoon or movie. But brands that hope to become a part of their customers' lives must evoke far more passion and loyalty than mere tearjerker advertising or tie-in marketing methods can deliver.

Often, understanding the emotional bond we have with brands or products is as simple as looking in the mirror and turning back the clock. Baby boomers, the most powerful consumer generation ever, recall with startling clarity and almost fanatical devotion their childhood playthings and adolescent pastimes. And they willingly spend big bucks on eBay or at the local kitsch boutique to recapture the artifacts of their youth. From *Lancelot Link* lunch boxes to "Mystery Date" board games and from Easy-Bake Ovens to Farrah Fawcett posters, what was once the cast-off clutter of neighborhood yard sales is now the time-capsule treasure hunted by a generation defined as much by its acquisitions as by its accomplishments.

Maybe that's why Carter's has had such success with its Real Love line of nursery products. Introduced in 1999, the charmingly offbeat collection is based on the colorful animals drawn by the late Beatle, John Lennon. Many of the items in the line play the tune "Imagine" in an updated version of a baby boomer's lullaby, putting boomers back in touch with their youth even while they bring the next generation into the world.

And it's certainly why a little Southern doughnut company called Krispy Kreme has been burning up the brand charts in recent years, opening stores from coast to coast and drawing crowds for its hot, fresh doughnuts on the basis of passionate word of mouth from those who grew up with the brand.

"It's not overly complicated. We try to give people a great experience—we try to give them what we call these 'magic moments,'" explains Stan Parker, Senior Vice President for Marketing at Krispy Kreme, referencing the company's brand promise, which was inspired by the happy recollections of loyal Krisby Kreme fans. "It's that idea—of magic and memory—that inspires our brand culture."

> WE TRY TO GIVE PEOPLE A GREAT EXPERIENCE . . . WHAT WE CALL THESE "MAGIC MOMENTS."
>
> **Stan Parker, Krispy Kreme**

The culture and commerce of the past forty years have in large part been driven by the brands that captured the spirit, embodied the dreams, and bottled the hope of the baby boomers and their own babies. From Calvin Klein Jeans to Starbucks Coffee, the WWF to Disney . . . the list is as self-evident as it is self-indulgent. Yet that which indulges the self enraptures the soul. And in the end inspires loyalty to the companies and brands that enable such compelling experiences. The brands and businesses that stake out a claim on the

---

✳ KRISPY KREME: HOT, FRESH MEMORIES

If you've experienced the soft, sugary, melt-in-your-mouth sensation of a Hot Original Glazed Doughnut, felt your heart skip a beat when that red neon "Hot Now" sign was on, or pressed your nose against the glass of a store window to watch doughnuts being made, then you know the magic of Krispy Kreme. And chances are, you've got some fond memories you're just dying to share with anybody who has yet to experience these simple joys.

Word of mouth has helped this once-sleepy Southern company bounce onto the national scene in the past decade as one of America's most beloved and charmed brands. With more than 200 stores in 33 states, and one in Toronto, the company is expanding, if carefully, by tapping the natural enthusiasm of its loyal customers and their endless delight at talking about doughnuts to anyone who will listen.

"It's such a powerful thing, when we go into a new market—people who have grown up with the brand are there, sharing their memories with everyone. So when we open, we've already had a lot of build-up, and a there's a lot of excitement around the opening," says Stan Parker, Senior Vice President of Marketing, recalling how Krispy Kreme fans in Denver camped out the night before a store opened there to be first in line for the tasty treats.

"When our loyal fans talk about Krispy Kreme, it starts with the product—the hot doughnut, that flavor when they'd first bite into it, and what it was like to watch the doughnuts being made—but then as they talk, they quickly move into a more emotional range, about what the brand has meant in their lives," Parker notes.

"People just associate Krispy Kreme with happy times. Whether it's a husband and wife who were honeymooning in Florida when they first discovered Krispy Kreme—and then ate there everyday—or someone remembering how they sold doughnuts to raise money for their Little League team, our consumers connect the brand with good things in their past."

The brand's ascendancy came a bit late, but it's making up for lost time. "We're an almost sixty-five-year-old company, but in many ways we're like a start-up," Parker says. "It wasn't until the early nineties when we started listening to customers talk about Krispy Kreme and realized that we had this enormous base of loyal consumers who had strong feelings around our brand." So strong, in fact, that the company has no need for traditional advertising, though it does have a Web site that attracts some 6000 emails a month (mostly from people eager to share their favorite doughnut memories).

A successful initial public offering of stock has capitalized on the company's growth spurt, but Krispy Kreme is remaining true to its homespun brand even as it expands into glitzy markets like New York City and Los Angeles. That careful evolution has involved transforming factory-focused outlets into cozy retail carry-outs, and switching on the now-famous red neon light to alert passersby that a fresh batch of doughnuts is ready for purchase.

What hasn't changed is the quality of the product itself, or the company's dedication to community giving. It offers discounts on doughnuts for fundraising efforts, and following the September 11th terrorist attacks (which destroyed a company store in the World Trade Center complex, though the employees all escaped) its stores distributed free doughnuts to blood donors around the country. "We didn't have to tell our employees to do that," Parker notes. "They just did. Because giving is a strong part of our brand culture."

And so is a loyal army of fans, whose mouthwatering word of mouth is helping Krispy Kreme sell hot doughnuts like hotcakes from coast to coast.

future will do so only by homing in on the emotional drivers and experiential expectations of a new breed of demanding, sophisticated, and stimulus-hungry consumer.

The Second Demandment—**Inspire Me**—is about the alchemy of evocative branding that conjures forth consumer enchantment and devotion. The consumer's reaction may be irrational or deeply personal, heartfelt or tickled pink. But whatever the depth and breadth of the reaction, the result is a sort of soulful connection that makes us feel understood by and related to a company, place, persona, or product.

> ## IF YOU CAN CAPTURE THE IMAGINATION OF THE CONSUMER THEN YOU MAKE A CONNECTION.
> **Hilary Billings, RedEnvelope**

RedEnvelope, a gift company that hopes to change the way people give—and think about giving—seeks to mine the depths of emotional reactions in its consumers and those to whom they give RedEnvelope gifts. "If you can capture the imagination of the consumer so that their experience of shopping with you becomes more meaningful than just a convenient place to go buy something—that they actually feel that you have improved their lifestyle," says RedEnvelope CEO Hilary Billings; "then you make a connection."

✳ THE VOICE OF THE CUSTOMER
CONNECT WITH ME

To tell you the truth, I'm not sure how it happens. It's sort of an invisible thing. But when there's a connection, I feel it— sometimes in my gut, sometimes in my head, and occasionally in my heart. Maybe it's your photography, but I doubt it. Maybe it's your clever words, but I don't think I'm that easily wooed. Maybe it's that you stand for something I stand for. Whatever it is, when you connect with me, it makes me feel like you "get it" and more important, that you "get me."

So don't just try to grab my attention, seek a real connection with me.

And that means you must . . .

■ **Believe in something that matters.** Chances are, it'll be something that matters to me, too. An idea. An ideal, a cause, a passion. When you're fired up about what you believe in, I get fired up too. If you don't love what you do and if you don't believe in it, how in the world can you expect me to feel that way?

■ **Inspire me to inspire my kids.** I want my kids to share my passion, but it's got to trickle down from me. So don't stick your logo on stuff just to get your name in front of my family. I appreciate the Home Depot line of construction toys that even includes child-sized safety goggles. Their toys help to reinforce a unique connection between me and my kids, instead of force-fitting a logo onto a child-size package.

Experiences that put us in the spotlight, make us feel special, and engage us with a sense of involvement and wonderment are among the most compelling and memorable we can have. Walt Disney figured that out when he opened Disneyland in Anaheim, California, in 1955. The first "theme park," it transformed the traditional amusement park into a landscape of themes and dreams, with sections like Fantasyland, Frontierland, Adventureland, and Tomorrowland, which added cultural context to traditional amusements and enhanced the entertainment value of the park's rides, shows, and shops.

But long before Disney, mankind's natural commercial and social instincts gave rise to gathering places that engaged, entertained, and intermingled the masses. Society has evolved from the instinctual need of people to come together and enjoy each other's company with a shared sense of community and commerce.

Public marketplaces and county fairs date back to more ancient times, long serving as the magnet for buyers and sellers to mingle, sell, and swap while connecting with others like themselves. Today's modern shopping malls are merely the latest in the long evolution of communal market experiences, now taken to the next level as architects and planners create thematic or hometown atmospheres that give shopping centers a destination appeal extending far beyond the functional facets of buying and selling.

Easton Town Center, just outside of downtown Columbus, Ohio, has become a national model for such atmospherically sublime shopping experiences. The 1.5-million-square-foot "mass leisure time destination," as its developer, Steiner and Associates, calls it, includes shopping "districts" (such as the recently added Fashion District, home to a Victoria's Secret flagship store), as well as a 30-screen movie theater, a town-square-like outdoor public space where free concerts often are held, and an inviting blend of shops and restaurants for all tastes and interests. The sum of its parts equals a spend-a-day destination rather than a pass-through stop-and-shop spot, but one that draws more on old-fashioned feelings of community and leisurely exploration than on over-the-top entertainment zones.

Like malls and markets, fairs and events have evolved into public showcases for brands and their value—this was especially true in the twentieth century, when world's fairs became corporate carnivals where consumers would crowd into pavilions to experience the latest innovations and marketing messages of leading brands and companies. What began as a showcase for countries and their cultures became a display of commerce and commercialism.

THE VOICE OF THE CUSTOMER
CREATE THE THEATER

Create a special place that immerses me in another world. Help me escape from the reality of my life by whisking me away, dropping me into the middle of a new sensory adventure. And make me a star in the show, or at least give me a cool part to play in the action.

Here are some tips for making me feel included . . .

- **Design the set.** It could be the location, combined with perfect color palette. Or the way the furniture is arranged just so. Or the soft, evocative lighting. Or the music that I can't get out of my head. No matter how you do it, when you do it right there's a special feel, a real vibe that draws me in.

- **Put me in the action.** I feel like I'm really in the game when I'm playing around at NikeTown, coffee-bonding at Starbucks, or buying and selling on eBay. When I arrive in Las Vegas, I'm immediately immersed in the atmosphere. Sure, I know they want my money. But they've created an entire city worthy of it. As one giant themed attraction, it swoops me into its razzle-dazzle embrace by delivering the ultimate experience of hands-on excitement, risk, and over-the-top showmanship. And somehow I feel like a star

there myself, because it's all designed to keep me entertained. Even when I'm losing in Vegas, I feel like a winner.

■ **Show, don't tell.** Create ways for me to imagine what's
possible in my life by putting your stuff into the context
of a world I desire. IKEA is brilliant at this. As I stroll from
one living space to the next, I can test-drive a new living
room or kitchen and visualize a creative and inexpensive
makeover.

While world's fairs are largely a thing of the past, almost any public
event, from a pro football game to a small-town Fourth of July pa-
rade, has become an opportunity for brand inspiration, sponsorship,
and product placement that builds emotional bridges to consumers
wherever they go.

Perhaps it was inevitable that once its design aesthetics and func-
tionality came of age, the Internet would evolve into a new outlet
for commerce, brand expression, and human interaction. The Net
began as a military communications system that then grew into an
academic and cultural knowledge base and network; but the
graphical wonders of the World Wide Web soon transformed what
had been a relatively dry, text-only experience into a rich new
medium that, when done well, can reflect, extend, enhance, and
magnify the messages and offerings of a brand's other channels.
And in doing so it can thread together the emotional and inspirational connections that brands need to weave with their consumers
across channels.

Whether online or off, the winners of the inspiration game are those
that create engaging and immersive experiences and destinations
where consumers can interact with companies or brands. So, in part
taking a page from Disney, we've seen the emergence of distinctively

themed restaurants (the Hard Rock Café launched a thousand themed imitators), stores (from the athletic-shoe wonderland of NikeTown to the dinosaur-bone-bedecked Discovery Stores) and hotels (Las Vegas' strip offers everything from the Luxor's ancient Egyptian flair to the Bellagio's classical Italian elegance).

And while some of these may only be passing fancies or have jumped on the "experience" bandwagon at a time of glitzy glut and opportunistic overkill, some themes have stood the test of time and found ways to evolve and expand their experience.

Take the House of Blues idea. It evolved from the fictional world of the Blues Brothers characters—first created on *Saturday Night Live* by Dan Aykroyd and John Belushi, then later portrayed in two movies. The Blues Brothers phenomenon launched a House of Blues chain of nightclubs in New Orleans, Los Angeles, Las Vegas, and Orlando, and in other entertainment-oriented cities.

The company also books concerts at more then 250 venues in North America, Webcasts streaming media of concerts, and has even expanded into the hotel business, with a blues-themed hotel in Chicago that keeps guests and patrons rocking into the wee hours. What gives this particular theme such marketplace magnetism?

"The first thing that always comes to mind when we talk about the House of Blues is the authenticity of the experience," explains Rebecca Kotch, Vice President of Retail for House of Blues. "We've really jumped the hurdles of the 'themed restaurants' world . . . from the choice of the materials inside the building to the art to the over-all setting. It's sort of a living museum . . . that's representative of the musical spirituality and the message of the brand. People love to stay immersed in the whole other world," she says. "You don't feel like this is something that was just built in a box."

Beyond the themes of music and entertainment, the aesthetic aura of sheer magnetism and style is on the rise as an inspirational, almost ambient, experience leader. Being part of "the scene" has always been an intriguing draw for people seeking a sense of self (and self-importance), and New York City's 1970s nightclub scene and 1980s restaurant scene bestowed upon dancers and diners an ephemeral aura of celebrity and status. It's no wonder that one of the creators of Studio 54, Ian Schrager, would go on to spawn the next stylish experience trend: transforming old hotels into upscale boutique lodgings such as the Phillippe Starke–designed Paramount Hotel, just off Times Square in New York City, and the St. Martins Lane Hotel in London. A stream of cool and clever hoteliers have followed in his footsteps since, and on a chain scale the Westin's W Hotels offer a similar blend of sophisticated, whimsical postmodern design and high-level service. These pricey, lively lodgings now cater to business travelers and vacationers from coast to coast who are made to feel hipper and trendier simply by staying in a particular hotel.

EXPERIENCE DEVOID OF REAL EMOTIONAL CONNECTION IS HOLLOW. But experience devoid of real emotional connection is hollow; despite the first-blush fascination with entertaining or chic environments or experiences, brands need to build deeper and more multifaceted connections to consumers if they hope to win their loyalty.

When you think of brands that touch people way beyond the channel interaction, names like Disney and Hallmark immediately spring to mind. And well they should: As the gold standard of inspirational and emotional branding, they have helped create a world where brands and their associated products are seen as modern-day icons by consumers seeking some semblance of meaning in a world

✳ THE OPRAH EFFECT

In publishing circles they call it "the Oprah Effect," as if it were a force of nature capable of altering the landscape in an instant, like a tidal wave or an earthquake. In a way, it is. When TV talk show host Oprah Winfrey announced on September 27, 1996, that she was forming an on-air book club "to get the whole country reading again," she set off a cultural avalanche that roared through the world of words.

The first selection of Oprah's book club was, Jacquelyn Mitchard's *The Deep End of the Ocean.* It had been published the previous June to good reviews and a respectable print-run of 100,000 copies. Not bad for a first novel. But within two days of Oprah's announcement, Mitchard's book was topping the bestseller lists, and its publisher, Viking, had pumped out 640,000 copies to serve the suddenly insatiable Oprah readership.

As Oprah's book club became a national obsession, viewer testimonials, letters, and emails poured in from women (her primary audience) who were rediscovering the joy of reading. And book clubs, long a social tradition among the literary set, suddenly were sprouting up everywhere, in homes and offices, bookstores, and coffeehouses. Reading had suddenly come out of the closet, and the bestseller lists were no longer the sole domain of genre superstars and diet gurus.

The Oprah Effect has not only changed America's reading habits; it has also significantly influenced the way fiction is published and marketed. Hitting the publishing world at a time when slow-moving titles were briskly marched off to the no-man's land of the remainder tables, the Oprah Effect has meant that promising titles which previously had gone unnoticed have been dusted off and prettied up, as publicists have scrambled to appeal to Winfrey's quirky tastes for lesser-known authors and slightly older books.

The Oprah Effect has gone through a few pendulum swings along the way, pushed back and forth in equal measures by its defenders and detractors. Even while readers and writers have sung its praises, elitist essayists have sniped and sniffed at the mass-media appeal of her reading groups, derisively envisioning an army of dull-eyed couch potatoes trudging dutifully to the local superstore for their monthly reading assignment stamped with the "Oprah's Book Club" logo. Falling into the latter camp, author Jonathan Franzen snubbed her selection of his book *The Corrections* (2001), claiming that her audience might not be up to the task of reading his lengthy tome. He later revisited his decision, but by then Oprah had decided not to feature him, after all.

Oprah has made the world a better place for almost everyone who loves books. And that is in no small part due to her promotion of reading as a life-affirming act of personal evolution and communal connection.

In the spring of 2002, Oprah announced that she was ending the book club as a regular feature on her talk show. After a six-year run, she said, "It has become harder and harder to find books on a monthly basis that I feel absolutely compelled to share." But the impact of her book club will live on in the new community of readers she has inspired.

cluttered with too much information and opportunity and too little context and guidance.

It's no surprise that both Disney and Hallmark came of age during the early twentieth century, when innovations in the realm of mass media were building new pathways to the hearts of an emerging modern consumer. Likewise, it seems only fitting that the late twentieth century saw the ascendancy of charismatic personalities, or "living brands," like Martha Stewart and Oprah Winfrey, who craftily serve up mass-market inspiration with individual flair and motivational messages.

In that funny way history has of doubling back on itself, it was the mass-marketing of entertainment and emotional bonding characteristic of the early century that brought us Disney and Hallmark, just as it was the need for a return to a personal connection that led us down the path to the living rooms and talk-show sets of Martha and Oprah.

The marketing powerhouses that are Martha and Oprah serve as inspirational guides for their legions of mostly female fans who seek beauty, peace, insight, or validation through the programming, publishing, and packaging of these secular saints of self-evolution. Their personalities and magnetism are so strong that they bridge the gap between mass culture and individual attention, making their followers feel special and inspired, yet part of something greater than themselves.

Motivation can come from different sources, for different needs. Superstar lifestyle gurus are cultural motivators for self-evolution; our mentors and coaches, friends and family are the everyday motivators who give us a reason to get up in the morning, keep us going all day and push us forward, step by step, to be better and try harder. The cultural motivators make us *want* to do more by holding up an image of what we could be, do, or achieve if only we would follow their lead; the personal motivators are there beside us as a part of our lives every day, cheering (or goading) us on to actually accomplish those goals.

The most effective cultural motivators are those who also provide inspirational empowerment and thus serve as personal motivators. Oprah's *O* magazine provides just this sort of ongoing support, giving her fans a monthly dose of reading that mirrors the message of her television show but then goes several levels deeper with in-depth topical features, real-people profiles, and you-can-do-it tools to improve their lives. Her magazine bridges the gap between her weekday hour of inspiration and the everyday lives of her fans by providing tangible, actionable resources that reinforce her living brand by delivering on its promise of self-evolution.

✳ VOICE OF THE CUSTOMER
MOTIVATE ME.

Sometimes I just need a little boost. A motivational jump-start. A push to get me going, to do something I know I should do but can't muster the initiative to do on my own. I guess in some way I'm looking for the parent we've all dreamed of—supportive, yet firm. Understanding, yet encouraging. Are you up to it?

Here's how to rev me up . . .

■ **Meet me where I am.** Sometimes it's hard to get started because I see too much work up ahead. When the next steps are too overwhelming, or you're too advanced for me, I get intimidated and forget it all together. Invite me into your world by recognizing what level I'm at right now—a newbie, a pro, or somewhere in between—and give me the tools I need to move on to the next stage.

■ **Help me see a better me.** Create the aspiration, and help me pursue my dream of getting from here to there. Recognize that I may not be as evolved, as in shape, as fast, as experienced, or as skilled as you are (yet). Acknowledge that this is okay. But show me the way, and encourage me along the path, the way Quaker Oatmeal does when it shows me real people who've lowered their cholesterol by eating their cereal, or the way Oprah's "Make the Connection" fitness program has helped me get moving again.

■ **Keep me going.** Even the smallest setback can be demotivating. If I get off track, know that I'm bound to need some encouragement to pick myself up and get back on my feet again. *Self* magazine makes it easy for me to stick with the dream through its annual fitness series that takes readers through a long-term plan for training and healthy eating. They keep me motivated month after month, instead of simply publishing a couple of pages on leg lifts and calling it a day.

Martha and Oprah, along with other living brands from Richard Simmons to Deepak Chopra, offer inspiration and self-actualization through doing (gardening, baking, exercising, decorating), thinking (reading, discussion, meditation), or simply being (meditation, self-acceptance, and simplification).

This need of ours for motivational gurus may be the result of living in a society in which rapidly developing technology and the relentless pace of everyday life have separated us from a sense of personal purpose, place, and meaning in the larger world. No longer do we rely on a shared bloodline or common-property line, a similar social class, race, or religion as our only conduit connecting us with "our own kind." Instead, we now often cheer our victories and drown our sorrows in the virtual company of like-minded enthusiasts who share our beliefs, passions, and interests. In essence, the boundaries of community have been both expanded and blurred; physical proximities have assumed less meaning as new kinds of cultural connections have been forged via the Internet and mass media.

In our global village we may still view ourselves as Christians or Jews, Southerners or New Yorkers, doctors or dancers, but we also define ourselves as snow-boarders or runners, cancer survivors or expectant mothers, Harley-Davidson buffs or Longaberger Basket collectors. It's not that we've abandoned meaningful connections with long-established institutions, it's simply that we've expanded our network of possibilities. And companies now are candidates for inclusion in that community, as long as they reach out to their consumers in relevant and inspiring ways.

Where once we were awed by the works of Renoir and Rodin on display in art galleries, many people now take equal pleasure in browsing for T-shirts, tote bags, and note cards emblazoned with images of those and other artists' works, for sale in the beautifully designed museum shops that share the same aesthetics as the museums themselves. And with even churches and temples adding coffee bars to their properties, members who come to worship now stay to chat with each other over a cappuccino instead of heading off after the prayer service to a secular Starbucks.

While many people view Western culture as crassly materialistic, our commercialism is a by-product of our industrialization. The transformational technologies and life-enhancing brands and products that have emerged in the past century (and the ensuing marketing and advertising associated with them) have led us to bond with the things that enable us to explore and enjoy the ideas and ideals to which we are devoted.

In this sense, the growth of corporate philanthropy and cause-related marketing can be mapped back to our search for meaningful connections with companies that go beyond the merely material. And giving simply feels good, not only to consumers but also to associates, investors, and anyone who connects with a company that's known for its good deeds.

"These kinds of programs, with a commitment to philanthropy and women's issues, resonate with our associates," notes Paul Charron, CEO of Liz Claiborne, which actively raises funds and promotes a program called "Love Is Not Abuse" to help women and at-risk teens in abusive relationships.

"We don't broadcast all the things we do because I just think it's unbecoming," Charron says. " But we are also not bashful about using our influence to get things done. It's just responsible corporate citizenship . . . and good business."

One of the good things to come out of the terrorist attacks on America is that we have seen how companies can make a difference through their public commitment to helping communities rebuild in any way possible, from providing clothes and food to rescue workers, and supplying pet food for displaced animals, to setting up support networks, college funds, and other long-term assistance for victims' families.

But businesses don't need to wait for a crisis to prove that they care about more than the bottom line. Savvy companies like Avon reach past their consumers' wallets and into their hearts by dedicating resources to causes that matter in the lives of those who bond with their brand.

Avon has been a leader in cause-related marketing efforts for breast cancer since the early 1990s—the Avon Breast Cancer Crusade, begun in 1993, has raised more than $150 million to fight the disease. The Avon Web site also offers a wealth of information about breast-cancer detection and treatment. And in 2001, as part of its Kiss Goodbye to Breast Cancer campaign, the company released a fundraising line of lipsticks with shade names such as Triumph, Strength, and Faithful Heart. For a company built by and for women (from the sales force to the customers), it's the right cause with the right message: We care about our customers and their lives.

THE VOICE OF THE CUSTOMER
HAVE A HEART.

I know about the importance of giving. It's just that I'm a little lax sometimes. But when you donate to a cause you believe in—when you put your money or resources where your mouth is—it sends a powerful message. One, that you're for real. And two, that perhaps I should do the same. Here's how to make a difference with me by making a difference in the world. . . .

- **Give where it counts.** Don't jump on the latest charity bandwagon. Be sure your cause relates to my life and to the business you're in. For instance, Target gives back 2 percent of its earnings to local organizations from purchases made with its card. That program makes me feel

like I'm making a difference right here where I live (and it
makes me feel better about my purchases!).

■ **Charity is more than checkbook-deep.** Get creative in
  your contribution. Donate supplies and services to organizations in need. Share available meeting rooms in your
  office with community groups. Or give your staff time off,
  to tutor kids or do other community work.

While a well-crafted, cause-related marketing campaign can reap
great benefits for companies, even those that come late to the game
can, in a moment of glory, grab the spotlight and win the hearts of
consumers with an act of unexpected largesse.

Such was the case in September 2001, when Amazon.com—which
wasn't particularly known for its philanthropy—transformed its
homepage into a donation drive for the American Red Cross in the
wake of the terrorist attacks on New York and Washington. In a
week, Amazon's campaign raised more than $6 million in disaster
relief. While other dot-coms followed suit (Yahoo! raised more than
$13 million in a similar fashion), Amazon was the first out of the
gate, and gained enormous publicity and public goodwill for its efforts. Amazon then upped the stakes at the holiday season by providing a way for consumers to purchase gift certificates that could
be donated to military servicemen and -women. Of course Amazon
was benefiting from those sales, but it made the company look good
by offering another innovative way to spread the love around to
those who were serving America in a
time of need.

Inspiration is the ultimate form of
communion between a company and
its consumers. Companies that touch

**INSPIRATION IS THE
ULTIMATE FORM OF
COMMUNION
BETWEEN A COMPANY
AND ITS CONSUMERS.**

the hearts, minds, souls, and spirits of their consumers deliver experiences that go beyond the commercial and transcend the trivial. They are deeply felt, genuine, and enchantingly memorable. True believers are not born: They are inspired. And so are loyal customers.

DEMANDMENT 02: **INSPIRE ME—SELF-EVALUATION**

Now that you've read this Demandment, see how you stack up. The checkpoints in this form reflect the key takeaways from the "Voice of the Customer" sections. Identify where your company could stand some improvement, and you'll have a shot at building bridges with the people who keep you in business.

2. INSPIRE ME	Excellent	Good	Poor
Connect with me.	Stand for something meaningful that touches consumers on an emotional level.	Touch consumers on an emotional level.	Failure to connect on an emotional level.
Create the theater.	Offer a sensory-driven environment that invites consumer participation.	Offer a sensory-driven environment.	Environment lacks sensory stimulation.
Motivate me.	Provide encouragement and stimulation for achieving self-enhancement or positive results.	Provide encouragement for achieving positive results.	Assume consumer will be self-motivated by features and benefits.
Have a heart.	Actively support philanthropic organization that is relevant to customers.	Sometimes support philanthropic organization that is relevant to customers.	Don't practice philanthropy.

The Third Demandment

make it easy

LET'S FACE IT: We live in an era of unprecedented progress and a state of constant confusion. We're burned out by the daily grind and freaked out by the nightly news. Somehow, despite all our modern marvels and time-saving devices, our work-week has actually expanded; we spend more time running more errands, and we have fewer hours of rest and relaxation.

For all the tools and technologies designed to increase our productivity (and presumably decrease our efforts), according to the International Labor Organization the United States is now the hardest-working nation in the industrial world—leapfrogging even

Japan in average hours worked. And Americans work an average of eight weeks longer a year than Europeans. While our physical labor may have decreased, thanks to automation and other wonders of modern advances, the brain drain is swirling ever faster as we try to keep up with the demands of our new knowledge-based economy.

Part of the problem: We're drowning in niche products, tech toys, and information glut. Captives of our multiple choices and wide-open lines of communication, we now dread opening our office email in the morning, knowing it will be clogged with messages that we'll never get around to reading. And when we get home in the evening we face a pile of mail-order catalogs, credit-card offers, and sales circulars—the average American household is inundated with 150 pieces of junk mail a month—that have come to us from companies which seem to know everything about us (except that we hate junk mail). Then we turn on the TV and get bombarded by endless channels of news, sports, and entertainment. We surf the Web and we're faced with millions of sites and billions of options. It's simply too much, and it never seems to end.

THE BOTTOM LINE FOR CONSUMERS IS PRETTY BASIC: DON'T COMPLICATE OUR LIVES.

The bottom line for consumers is pretty basic: Don't complicate our lives. Hence the message of the Third Demandment is pretty basic, too: **Make It Easy.** And unlike so much else in our lives, it really is as simple as it sounds. Consumers want things fast, easy, and understandable. They want to find what they want when they want it. They want to wait in as few lines as possible, for as short a time as possible. They want products and services so intuitive that no directions or assembly are required; or if instructions are needed, ones that are streamlined and easy to follow. It's about less complexity, more utility, and ultimately the improvement, simplification, and edification of everyday life.

It's no wonder consumers are demanding less excess and more ease. The phrase "shop 'til you drop" takes on new meaning when you realize that, with some five-and-a-half billion square feet of retail space spread across the United States—that's 20 square feet for every man, woman, and child in the United States—we're simply "overstored." And what goes into all that square footage can be just as overwhelming.

THE VOICE OF THE CUSTOMER
SIMPLIFY MY DECISION.

I have to make so many decisions in the course of the day, I'd like some of them to get easier. I'm often overwhelmed by the sheer volume of choices, especially for stuff like cereal or shampoo. And I can't remember the last time I felt confident picking a cold medicine from that arsenal of options on the drugstore shelf that makes me wish I had a medical degree just to figure out what I need. Especially when I'm making a big financial commitment for a home, a car, mutual funds, or a computer, I want my decision to be easier so that I can just get on with it.

Here's how to ease my load by making it easier for me . . .

- **Give me fewer, but better, choices.** I know it sounds funny, but sometimes I actually don't want to consider a gazillion choices. So when you package things together for me, it's a kind of shorthand to help me make a fast decision. I like Chipotle, a Mexican fast-food eatery that's owned by McDonald's, because they understand I want fresh ingredients and good food without a long wait or a long menu. To speed things along they have limited menu choices, but they let me customize my order by choosing the ingredients for my burritos or tacos as I move through the line while they make my meal.

- **Top-ten lists.** They're not just for Dave Letterman anymore. Create a top-ten list of what's jumping off the shelves, or find other ways of showing me what's hot now and why. I figure if everyone else is buying something it's probably worth a try, so give me a hint about what's got the buzz. For instance, I've come to depend on the *New York Times'* bestseller list for good reads, and I love the fact that most of the big bookstore chains now put it where I can see it (and offer me discounts when I buy books on the list).

- **Single servings, please.** I got hooked on wrapped cheese and disposable handi-wipes years ago. Now there are individually wrapped servings of peanut butter and jelly, disposable baby bibs, and facial cleansing cloths, just to name a few singletons. What do they have in common? One-time use and total convenience. Not that everything in this world should be disposable—I think recycling is a wonderful thing—but when it comes to cleaning up, packing lunch, or doing my beauty routine, every single timesaver counts.

Consumers now must navigate the football-field-length aisles of the super-supermarket, staring glassy-eyed at shelves of laundry detergents, tooth pastes, juices, and snacks marketed for every conceivable kind of consumer need. Our favorite brands have splintered into so many subproducts that it's hard to find the original formula we've used for years. It's no wonder: According to *The Progressive Grocer*, the number of supermarket stock-keeping units (SKUs) has doubled since the 1970s, when the average supermarket stocked some 15,000 SKUs. Today, most supermarkets have around 30,000 SKUs—and new supermarkets average closer to 45,000 SKUs. That's twice the stuff, but our basic needs haven't really changed all that much.

Yes, consumers demand options and choices, but they want ones that make their lives easier, not harder. Bigger, broader, and vaster product lines, created for the sake of seizing more shelf space or serving increasingly miniscule niche markets, can sometimes have the opposite rather than the intended effect on the average consumer: They get so overwhelmed that they're turned off of the brand and everything associated with it.

Today's consumers have short attention spans, and little patience with brands that don't reveal themselves right up front. Mysteries are fine for Agatha Christie readers, but people want to connect with companies that mean something to them, not spend an hour scratching their head about what a company actually does, or what its products are meant for.

People seek to *live* their lives, not *spend* their lives—they want their lives to move along with a meaningful flow, not be frittered away

PEOPLE SEEK TO *LIVE* THEIR LIVES, NOT *SPEND* THEIR LIVES.

with an endless array of learning curves, false starts, confusing devices, or overcomplicated transactions. Human beings haven't evolved nearly as quickly as our technologies, so we haven't yet adapted to the accelerated pace demanded of us by the complex information processing and skills associated with our own inventions and innovations. Faced with an ever-escalating need to catch up, keep up, or get ahead of new products, services, and trends, we

WE CRAVE SIMPLICITY AND EASE AS THE ANTIDOTE TO CONSTANT FRUSTRATION AND CONFUSION.

crave simplicity and ease as the antidote to constant frustration and confusion.

The companies that respect this simple truth will win the hearts, minds, and trust of consumers exhausted by too many gadgets, news sources, catalogs, product choices, and service options.

✳ THE VOICE OF THE CUSTOMER
LET ME PICK IT UP.

Sometimes I know what I want before I get there, so let me get the business part of the deal over with on the phone, by FAX, or online. There's a state-of-the-art movie theater in downtown Columbus, the Drexel Arena Grand, that not only lets me buy tickets online for hot movies (and avoid a sell-out situation); I can even reserve specific seats in the primo balcony section, so if I arrive late with my family we can all still sit together.

Maybe that's why the idea of car-sharing is catching on in America at last. Popular in Europe since the late 1980s, the trend toward sharing a limited fleet of rental vehicles among a pool of members is hitting the big time in the United States at last. Scrappy little start-ups with snappy titles like the Boston-based Zipcar, founded in 2000—and now expanding to Washington, D.C., and New York City—are revving their engines at the start of a new movement in transportation conservation. The companies use the Internet to facilitate membership sign-up and car reservation, and to help urbanites do away with the hassles and cost of car ownership or longer-term rental when they just need to run a few errands. The fleets are even covered by group insurance, so members needn't carry their own policies.

✳ IT TAKES AN HOUR ... OR A CAR

It seems like everybody's in a hurry to be someplace else. While this is hardly a Zen way of living, companies that understand their customers' need for speed and can deliver quality services or products to time-crunched consumers are thriving now more than ever.

And we're not just talking about drive-through burger joints, one-hour eyeglasses, slick oil-changes, or 60-minute film developing. Everyone from morticians to musicians is getting into the fast and efficient act.

Here's a sampling of some of the more creative products and services that go-getters can get on the go, in this day and age:

In an hour or less, you can . . .

- Diagnose a bacterial infection (Infection Diagnostic: *www.infectio.com*)

- Perfect the art of tying a necktie (with "The Tie Video," from Video Solutions)

- Learn to Speed Read (Speed Read America: *www.speedread.org*)

- Learn to play guitar (Gib Kerr's One Lesson Only Complete Guitar Course: *www.gibkerr.com*)

- Paint a watercolor (using Patrick Seslar's book *The One-Hour Watercolorist*)

In a car, you can drive-through to . . .

- Tie the knot at A Little White Chapel's Tunnel of Love Drive-Through (Las Vegas, NV).

- Mourn a loved one at Harvey Funeral Chapel's drive-through funeral services (Phoenix, AZ)

- Get caffeinated and cultured at the CARpuccino drive-through coffee shop and art gallery (Allentown, PA)

- Fill up your scuba-diving air tanks at Buddy Dive Resort's drive-through air-fill station (in Bonaire, Netherlands Antilles)

Though they use the Internet to ease the way, Zipcar is far from virtual or invisible to its customers—they sprinkle their fleet cars throughout cities in easy-to-reach locations, instead of in barricaded airport lots. And communications are equally accessible—in fact, Zipcar co-founder and CEO Robin Chase is known for responding to customer emails herself, creating a personal connection with members that helps to point up the community aspect of Zipcar membership.

Consumers, who are now more empowered than ever to vote with their wallets and leave brands in the dust with a single click of the mouse or slam of a door, view their favorite everyday conveniences as role models for what they expect—and demand—from every brand, every service, and every place of business: ease and speed.

The millions of people who drive through Wendy's for their lunch, swing by the ATM for cash, and drop off their film at a one-hour processing kiosk are losing their patience with overly complex technologies, badly designed check-outs, and confusing customer-service loops. If your company can't help them get in and get out and get on with their lives, then get out of their way, because they'll stampede right over you on the way to the exit.

THE VOICE OF THE CUSTOMER
MAKE IT FAST, OR FORGET IT.

You've probably already figured this out, but if you haven't, here's the scoop: I haven't got all day here! Let me get in and get back out as fast as I want to move, especially if you're selling me everyday stuff that can be a chore for me to shop for all the time. McDonald's nailed it with their order-by-number meals and speedy drive-through service. And grocery stores are in on the action with fresh, prepared meals and grab-and-go aisles located near their entrances, so I don't spend an hour looking for a loaf of bread.

Ready to pick up the pace? Here are some swift hints. . . .

- **Shorten my wait.** Speed is the name of the game. So don't make me stand in a line, especially a long one, because I'll get grumpy and impatient thinking about all the other things I could be getting done elsewhere and why you don't seem to understand that.

- **I want fewer steps . . . for everything.** I love Amazon's "1-Click" ordering that lets me buy stuff fast, without having to type in all my information every time I buy from them. And I like how Pizza Hut remembers my last order when I call, and knows where I live without having to ask for my address or directions. I'm getting used to that kind of ease; so if a store keeps asking me for the same info

over and over again, the only time it's saving me is in
how much faster I'll get frustrated with them.

■ **Beep me to keep me.** If I have to wait—whether it's for an
oil change at your garage, or a table at your busy restaurant—don't leave me sitting there in limbo, waiting for
you to give me the green light. Do what the Cheesecake
Factory does: Hand me a beeper and let me wander the
mall or go make some phone calls while you're doing
your thing, then buzz me when you're ready for me. It
helps me make the most of my time instead of leaving
me fidgeting and pacing in your lobby.

Not that consumers don't appreciate a bit of complexity in their
lives, if they can still be served quickly and efficiently, as in the case
of the Starbucks specialty coffee drinks. The Seattle-based coffee
chain that launched a thousand sips might seem to have made its
greatest cultural mark by selling an indulgent array of variations on
the basic cup of joe, but in actuality Starbucks is a brand that's as
much about speed as it is about specialty.

The company's success is based in part on its *baristas'* ('coffee-
makers') ability to fulfill complex drink orders with factorylike
speed and craftsmanlike flair, all the while accompanied by the cof-
fee-scented cacophony of hissing espresso machines and loudly
grinding beans. Such efficient drink artistry is only one part of the
whole experience, which also includes the plush seating and socializ-
ing areas, the music that's played (and sold on special Starbucks-
branded CDs), and the array of intriguing gewgaws on sale that vary
from location to location.

"We recognize there's a duality," explains Steve O'Neill, Director of
Concept Development for Starbucks. "You want highly efficient

brewers who can crank out the beverages and keep the line short and so on and so forth. But at the same time there's theater associated with that activity that's extremely important to us. That's something we think about all the time. And so as we study and understand . . . how to get faster . . . we have to view it through the filter of not losing the drama."

Innovating for continued customer satisfaction remains an important task for Starbucks, which celebrated its thirtieth anniversary in 2001. That same year the company introduced the Starbucks Card, which lets patrons load up a card with money and then draw against the balance for purchases without having to dig for spare dollars whenever the latte lust strikes. Cardholders can also register online to monitor their accounts, add more money to the card, or shop for gifts. The company is also testing phone-ahead ordering in certain markets, to speed up the process for morning commuters frustrated with long lines when the office clock is ticking.

When it comes to making it easy, there's no better proving ground (or opportunity for failure) than the digital world. So it should come as no surprise that the majority of new Internet users are coming online via America Online. The leading Internet service provider (ISP), AOL has more than 30 million registered users, and it didn't get there by simple luck or aggressive acquisition tactics alone. The company's strategy of flooding the market early and often with free CDs bearing AOL software and bombarding the airwaves with advertising has certainly helped gain it awareness among consumers.

But it takes more than mere marketing muscle to keep members signing up and logging on. From the outset AOL was designed for *technophobes*, not technophiles. The account set-up, navigation, site design, labeling, content, and assortment of stores and media partners are all geared toward a hesitant audience of computer newbies.

✳ THE FAST-FOODING OF AMERICA

Perhaps it started when Swanson Frozen Foods introduced the TV dinner in 1954. Or maybe the drive-through burger joint made it so. Then again, it may have been the advent of the microwave oven that kicked us into gear. Whatever the source of the inspiration, Americans are addicted to a life of convenience, especially when it comes to food.

You only have to peek inside our cupboards and pantries to see the change afoot in our lives. According to the latest version of a study produced every five years by Kraft Foods' Kraft Kitchens (who else but the macaroni-and-cheese whizzes would study this sort of thing?), Americans are stocking up on fewer and fewer staples of cooking, and filling their shelves instead with more and more ready-to-eat and easy-to-make packaged food products.

This study of more than 1700 households nationwide revealed that while only 44 percent of American households stocked butter and 55 percent kept milk on hand, a whopping 72 percent of households had spaghetti or vermicelli at the ready.

These ingredients, of course, add up to a tasty treat for companies like Kraft. HMR (Home Meal Replacement—granted, not exactly a consumer-friendly term) is one of the fastest-growing sectors in the food industry. No major grocery store is without a prepared food section offering everything from sushi to fried chicken to fresh fruit salad; and some mega-markets, like Giant Eagle, create a whole café environment around their carry-out meals department, encouraging shoppers to dine in during their shopping trip.

With consumers spending more than $100 billion on carry-out convenience foods, it's no wonder stores are looking for ways to keep them coming back for more.

People are also looking for products that offer more "creative convenience," such as upscale take-out meals with a restaurant taste and presentation, to re-create that dining-out-while-dining-in experience. This European trend has recently jumped the Atlantic, spawning New York City's Prete à Manger ("ready to eat"), which offers gourmet-to-go food that even the most finicky urban diner would be proud to serve guests.

Also on the rise are carry-outs that let consumers do the final prep at home—from the prepackaged frozen stir-fry dinners sold in the grocery store to the take 'n' bake gourmet pizzas, lasagna trays, or prefilled desserts prepared and sold through carry-outs, then taken home by consumers for the final cooking and serving.

Whether we dine in at our local grocery store or carry out a prepared meal, there's no going back: America's food culture is all about convenience. And the companies finding the greatest success are those taking the fastest route possible to their consumers' hearts—by going through their stomachs at mach speed.

And to this day the Virginia-based company's family-friendly personality and consumer-centered design and "easy to use" corporate mantra remains the key to the fast-growing media empire's success.

THE VOICE OF THE CUSTOMER
MAKE IT USABLE AND USEFUL.

Some things are easy to use. Others are useful—they serve a good purpose. But not everything is both, and I find that really frustrating. Why should I bother with something that's easy to use if I have no reason to use it? And likewise, if something is useful but hard to use, what's the point? Whatever you're trying to sell me should be both—useful and usable. Like a travel mug that keeps coffee hot and is easy to grip and sip while in transit. Or a medical Web site that has helpful information and lets me easily search for what I'm looking for.

Here's how to make yourself useful . . .

- **More isn't better.** Nothing ruins a great product like too many features. Beautiful design loses its charm if it stops me from doing what I'm trying to do, or if I can't figure out what to do in the first place. Coolness only goes so far if it has no other purpose. But a smart design feature, like easy-to-open medicine bottles for arthritis sufferers, is always welcome.

- **If it ain't broke, don't fix it**. New doesn't always mean improved. I may have liked the old product just fine—so even if you're planning to update your stuff, don't forget what I liked about it in the first place. Remember when New Coke came out? They had to re-release the classic version to satisfy loyal drinkers who still preferred the less-sweet original. It's fine to improve on a good thing;

just don't destroy what was good about it in the first place, in the name of progress.

■ **Keep it in the family.** If you've got a great line of products that works well together, make sure they look the part. I love the OXO series of hand-held kitchen utensils because they're easy to use and they all have the same look and feel. So when I'm shopping they stand out, making it easy to add to my collection.

The backlash against complexity is happening online and off, with consumer-centric design in all areas, from print to interactive to the retail environment, replacing the razzle-dazzle of bells-and-whistles products and services that helped puff up the NASDAQ bubble and widen the digital divide. When the bubble burst, it let loose a gust of hot air that wiped out plenty of companies lacking in truly useful products or services. The post-bubble survivors are those with proven value to their customers who show some real promise for the future.

THE BACKLASH AGAINST COMPLEXITY IS HAPPENING ONLINE AND OFF.

Now consumers are at the helm of their own destiny more than ever before, and as the usability wave continues to grow, smart companies are reexamining their products and packaging, information design, and transaction processes, as well as customer-service touchpoints and online and off-line experiences, all with an eye toward making it simpler for consumers to do, buy, and enjoy more.

As consumers demand more useful, usable, meaningful products—and less fluff, stuff, and nonsense from companies—the money that's spent on, packaging, marketing, and advertising will be wasted if it doesn't support simply better products, services, and experiences. Give your consumers a break by making their lives easier and they'll make it easier for your company to succeed.

DEMANDMENT 03: **MAKE IT EASY—SELF-EVALUATION**

Now that you've read this Demandment, see how you stack up. The checkpoints in this form reflect the key takeaways from the "Voice of the Customer" sections. Identify where your company could stand some improvement, and you'll have a shot at building bridges with the people who keep you in business.

3. MAKE IT EASY	Excellent	Good	Poor
Simplify my decision.	Feature a well-defined offering and a framework for rapid decision making.	Feature a well-defined offering.	Provide too many choices.
Let me pick it up.	Accept phone and online orders for pickup at physical location.	Accept phone orders for pickup at physical location.	Product purchase and pick-up cannot be separate transactions.
Make it fast, or forget it.	Consumers rarely have to wait, and systems are in place to expedite repeat customers.	Consumers occasionally have to wait.	Consumers often have to wait.
Make it usable and useful.	Products or services are easy to use, and consumers can't live without them.	Products or services are fairly easy to use, and important to consumers.	Products or services are the sources of confusion or frustration.

The Fourth Demandment

put me in charge

"CHARGE!" is more than a battle cry for credit card shoppers—it's a driving force for consumers who now, more than ever, want to be in charge of every aspect of their lives. Having tasted the freedom (and learned to accept the risks and responsibilities) that come with opportunity, choice, information, and customization, people now demand control over every twist and turn of their transactions. They want control of the process and its outcome, from where and how they shop, buy, and pay, to the ways in which their information is collected, stored, and used, and the kinds of communications they receive from companies.

Control is the key to success in the Fourth Demandment, **Put Me in Charge.** In an age where people have more choices than they can absorb, taking charge of the buying process at an earlier stage helps them feel empowered rather than overpowered by the experiences that lead to their purchase experience or service commitments. And companies that give their customers a sense of control over their options and transactions are sending a message that they value, respect, and want to serve them as unique individuals with unique needs.

Of course, consumers have always owned the final move in the transaction game. No amount of clever marketing or superior salesmanship can change the fact that it's the consumer's hand on the wallet, on the keypad, or on the phone disconnect button. But now, more than ever, consumers are enjoying a new kind of control that bridges the gap and extends the boundaries of their two historical moments of control: the choice to enter a channel (either literally or virtually), and the decision to sign a sales slip or agree to a service.

But just before, in between, and after those entry and exit points are control zones where companies have traditionally kept the hand on the till. From limiting access to particular channels or ways of interacting with support, to visual merchandising, product selection, pricing, messaging, providing decision support to customer service, and even the follow-up communications, these elements of the consumer experience are all in play when someone is actively engaged within a company's control zone. And until recently, they were largely out of the consumer's sphere of influence.

Companies still have a strong measure of control in these areas, but consumers have gotten a taste of freedom and empowerment in recent years through experiences that range from setting their own prices on airline tickets to mixing their own customized CDs at music stores. Even such low-tech do-it-yourself experiences as using

NETFLIX: DVDS TO YOUR DOORSTEP

One of the best ways to put consumers in charge is to give them more control over an experience they have routinely found to be frustrating. Like, for instance, stopping by the local movie-rental store on a Friday night, ready to stock up on hot flicks for the weekend, only to find that the top DVDs are already rented out. You stand around, hoping that somebody will return a movie you've been looking for, but other people already are ahead of you on the wait lists. Why bother?

Enter Netflix. This San Jose, California, company, founded in 1997, has made a big splash by taking most, if not all, of the annoyance out of the DVD rental experience. They've simplified and streamlined the process by letting members rent three DVDs at a time for a flat monthly fee. No late fees apply, but since people can't rent more DVDs until they've sent back what they have, it's sort of a self-policing principle. And all the transactions are handled online and by mail.

Sure, red-hot DVDs sometimes still do get rented out faster than members can order them. But with such a vast selection—over 10,000 titles to choose from—it's easier to find something to watch.

Members use the Netflix site to store their DVD wish list, and then the company sends out the requested disks. After watching a DVD the member just pops it into the postage-paid return envelope, and the next DVD on the member's list gets sent out in the mail. The Web site features a searchable database of movie titles, reviews by members, and suggestions of other rental titles that relate to the same category, so it offers far more decision support than your typical movie-rental experience.

And by using the Internet to take orders, and the U.S. mail system for distribution, the company doesn't have to support the costs of storefront staff or infrastructure and yet members have easy, 'round-the-clock ordering access and doorstep delivery.

The downside? Members have to wait for their orders to arrive in the mail, instead of walking out of a rental store with a DVD in hand. But once they get used to ordering in advance, the system seems to work very well.

Until true video-on-demand becomes widely available, Netflix seems to be the next best thing. With 300,000 paying subscribers and growing fast, it has caught on, in part, by giving consumers greater control over the variety of selection and length of rental, plus the ease of online ordering and postal delivery. That's a one-two-three-four punch.

a salad bar or a self-serve gas pump are small but meaningful moments in which consumers feel much more in control of the how, what, when, and where (as opposed to just the if) of buying.

> AS LONG AS WE KEEP THE CONSUMER IN MIND, WE WILL ALWAYS BE WHERE WE ARE.
>
> **Brian McNamara, Procter & Gamble**

Clearly, technology has played a part in giving consumers a greater sense of control—at least, with brands that understand the realities of what technology can and can't do for their consumers. "All those innovations would be useless if they weren't based in deep consumer understanding," notes Brian McNamara, Brand Manager for Procter & Gamble's Tide. "As long as we keep the consumer in mind and we make sure they're the boss, and they're #1, then we will always be where we are." The only danger of getting lost in the shuffle, says McNamara, is forgetting who the real boss is by straying from the consumer's best interest. "If we lose our way it will be because we do innovation for innovation's sake or technology for technology's sake. Then we're probably in big trouble."

And just as parents stand back, torn between pride and panic as their child first peddles away down the sidewalk on her own, so too when companies allow their consumers to take greater control of their experience it's an intimate moment of interdependence and independence. To fulfill their consumers' needs for autonomy, companies must come to view this empowerment shift as an opportunity to cede control in order to create a more trusting and loyal relationship with their consumers.

✳ THE VOICE OF THE CUSTOMER
GET OUT OF MY WAY!

Face it. Sometimes you're slowing me down or speeding me up when I'm not ready. You're acting like a control freak. And I've got things to do: stuff to cross off my list, errands to run, work to get done. So scoot over, I'm driving now! You just have to accept that sometimes I want to go it alone, because that's what works for my overscheduled, overcommitted, stress-filled life.

Get the picture? Here's how to bring my needs into focus . . .

- **Let me choose my path.** Don't force me down the path you want me to take. Fine, show off your new stuff if you must. But don't limit me to what you're pushing. I may want to see my old favorites. Go left, not right. Shop by color, size, or price, or brand, depending on what suits me (I can do that at BlueFly.com, and it's fabulous!). It all depends on my mood and my circumstance on any given day.

- **My pace is my own.** Even if I'm usually in a hurry, sometimes I like to slow down and explore. I may not even be in a buying mood, frankly, but just out surveying the territory. And I like moving at my own pace without pressure from you. So don't corner me for a test drive and a high-pressure pitch when I simply want to browse the lot. Don't shoo me away or push me to try or buy immediately. And please don't be disappointed if I decide not to sign on the dotted line today. Let me discover what you're about, and I may be back.

- **Let me go deep.** If my curiosity is piqued, let me dive below the surface. I might want to hear your expert staff explain the difference between whey and soy, watch a video about furniture stripping, or attend a workshop about investing. Or maybe I simply want to go online to dig. When I'm into something, I can't get enough information. I want to absorb as much as I can. I want to know as much as you do before I buy into what you're selling me. So serve me up a healthy portion of facts, figures, features, classes, news, tips, and useful databases, and I'll be smart enough to make the right choices for myself.

The landscape of consumer touch points and transaction turning points provides plenty of opportunities to give people control over key decisions along the way. But the more complex the transaction, the greater the likely number of changes in direction and control along the way. While some buying decisions are as simple as grabbing a magazine from a stand and paying the clerk, others—from negotiating the details of a custom-built home to selecting a hospital maternity ward—are far more complex and require many layers of decision support that lead to informed, empowered choices.

The more expensive the purchase, complex the decision, or layered the options, the more likely it is that a consumer is engaged in a transaction that will have a long-term impact on his or her life. A nervous young man buying a diamond engagement ring is doing more than splurging on a fancy piece of jewelry for his girlfriend—he's investing in a symbol of his love, desire for commitment, and hope for the future. And a pregnant couple shopping for a minivan is looking for more than a way to get around town—they're anticipating many years of baby seats and soccer games, family road trips, and school car pools.

Giving consumers greater control over a transaction puts them in greater control of their lives. People who feel in charge of these decisions are receiving a message from a company that says, in essence, "we're here to give you what you want and need, not just to sell you stuff we want you to buy."

GIVING CONSUMERS GREATER CONTROL OVER A TRANSACTION PUTS THEM IN GREATER CONTROL OF THEIR LIVES.

✳ THE VOICE OF THE CUSTOMER
DON'T TRAP ME.

Don't try to force me to spend time with you. Get rid of the dead ends that make me wish I'd sprinkled breadcrumbs just to find my way back out again. It doesn't matter if I'm at a cocktail party, a movie theater, a Web site, or supermarket, if

> I can't see the exit or a way back out, I feel trapped. That was
> how I felt the few times I went to Incredible-Universe, the
> electronics superstore that's since gone out of business. I
> had to scan my membership card just to get in the door, and
> then I had to navigate an obstacle course even when I just
> needed to buy a few blank videotapes. No wonder I stopped
> going there!

Thanks to manufacturing advances and tools that allow for product recommendations and configuration, people are beginning to expect a greater level of control and customization over even the simplest of products and services, from skin care products and cosmetics to athletic shoes and breakfast cereals.

A toe-tapping case in point: music. Since the early days of audiocassette recorders, people have been taping compilations of their favorite songs, making bootlegs of concerts, and swapping tunes with pals. Then came the advent of CD burners, make-your-own-CD music systems at retail and online stores, and ultimately, peer-to-peer (P2P) file-sharing sites like Napster that let millions of music fans find and download tracks from each other's computers free of charge. Suddenly, consumers who felt few qualms about taking a shortcut around piracy and copyright laws could create customized music collections for little or no money. The idea that "information wants to be free" became a battle cry for swappers, who saw their actions as akin to civil disobedience.

While computer software piracy has long been an issue, the arrival of Napster and its P2P-sharing kin opened a Pandora's Box of trouble, not for only the music industry, but also for virtually every creator, producer, or distributor of intellectual property, from Hollywood movie studios to New York book publishers. The upshot? Companies are developing new ways to meet the demands of this renegade consumer audience by offering free samples, wider assortments, and greater customization capabilities, even while working to strengthen laws against copyright infringement and to create better anti–file-sharing technologies. It may not stop the swapping, but the idea clearly is that by giving people more control over the products, they may not try so hard to share so much.

Of course, customization is nothing new—Burger King's "Have it your way" burger campaign long ago proved that companies can satisfy consumer appetites and demands by tapping into their personal preferences. While Burger King may have been first in line to tout its customizing services, many companies today frequently retool their offerings so as to give their consumers a more individualized, in-charge experience. From banks that offer personal check styles and à la carte financial services, to home furnishings stores that provide myriad configurations of furniture systems, the idea that the customer is always right—and now, always in control—is becoming more fully established in progressive merchandising circles.

Part of being in control means being able to transact however and wherever we want. This is at the heart of the Sixth Demandment—**24/7**—but it's also part of the control mission companies must adopt if they are to meet consumers' increasingly take-charge demands.

Multichannel integration is giving consumers more choices than ever before, about how and where to buy. And the more integrated the brands become, the greater number of ways that companies can offer consumers cross-channel services such as in-store returns for online purchases, gift certificates for use in any channel, and gift registries that stay in synch in every channel. When handled seamlessly, these experiences give consumers a sense that they can interact with a brand wherever they choose.

While it's been more common for brick-and-mortar institutions to go the click-and-mortar route, some Web-based pure players—from the dearly departed Garden.com to the more muscular Amazon.com—have taken the opposite route by adding catalog components to their channel offerings.

One such company is UncommonGoods, an up-and-coming e-retailer that specializes in creatively designed gifts (motto: "find anything but ordinary"). "Originally, I saw the Internet as a marketing vehicle that was vastly superior to a catalog. It could contain greater depth of information, it could be updated more frequently, cost-effectively display more products, and had no mailing costs," says CEO Dave Bolotsky, who founded UncommonGoods in 1999. "But I ignored one important detail: customer behavior. Elements of the Internet are still not very customer-friendly. We have tried our best to humanize and simplify the experience, but it is painfully slow on a 56K modem (given our image-intensive site), and a lot less comfortable than sitting back in an easy chair, flipping through a catalog, calling a toll-free number, and having someone else do the data entry for you. Also, the catalog is a very effective way of getting the attention of both existing and prospective customers."

When it comes to humanizing the virtual experience, online investment giant E*Trade has taken an even larger leap out of cyberspace, putting financial service centers into Target stores to extend its presence into the real lives of its investors. By adding this physical element to the E*Trade experience, the company gains the gravitas of a "real" financial player. In times of economic downturn, giving consumers a more tangible way to interact with their investments is likely both to strengthen its existing relationships and to build awareness among those who are still Web-shy about trading online.

Beyond access to multiple channels, the almighty dollar remains a powerful piece of the **Put Me in Charge** pie for consumers, who now want greater control over product and service pricing. Consumer desires and technological enablers have dovetailed in recent years, setting off price wars, frenzied consumer research, and new ways of marketing to savvy consumers on the lookout for a better deal. While research has shown that price alone is not as strong a motivator as traditionally thought, consumers who have the ability to research and compare product prices, benefits, and options expect to get the best possible deal for their money. And they're not happy when a company tries to sell them a lesser product or service for a greater price.

Air travel, with its post-deregulation fare wars, has long been a price-point irritant for travelers, who often found themselves sitting next to someone who had paid considerably less, or more, for an identical seat on the same flight. No wonder, then, that Priceline.com took off—at least, at first—like a supersonic jet in 1998: For the first time, consumers could literally set their own prices for flights, identifying what they were willing to pay and waiting to see if any seats were available for that price.

Priceline has struggled since its launch, in part because the company mistakenly gambled that consumers would go out of their way to bid and pay online for everyday goods such as groceries and gasoline with the same zeal with which they approached purchasing variable-price products such as airline tickets. Still, it showed that there was a market for consumer-set pricing in areas where prices traditionally vary widely anyway.

That's the power of the Web: It connects buyers and sellers in ways never before imagined. When the online auction site eBay was founded in 1995, it quickly transformed the Internet into the world's largest yard sale by giving individuals the tools to transact with each other as if they were just down the block. So now, when Mom sells her son's old collection of comic books, if he's lucky enough to be on eBay at the time he can snatch them up before somebody else does—even if he lives across the country.

Likewise, price-comparison tools such as the 'bots that scour the Internet for low prices and great deals have also helped to put consumers in the driver's seat as never before. Add this to the information empowerment wrought by the breadth and depth of research resources available to consumers at the click of a mouse or the touch of a phone pad, and you realize how much more bargaining strength today's consumers have even before they pull out their wallets.

Assuming, that is, that a company's Web site has given them what they really needed to make a decision, as opposed to just what a retailer wanted to spoon-feed them. "It's a tool. People get enamoured with the technology for technology's sake, and forget the fundamental of retail. And the fundamental of retail is 'Give the lady what she wants.' And what she wants isn't gigaflops of data," notes Dan Finkelman, Senior Vice President for Brand and Business Planning for The Limited, Inc., in speaking about how some companies fail their consumers by misunderstanding the Web's value.

"For retailers," Finkelman insists, "the Web did not revolutionize our thinking. It revolutionized our delivery. What I always wanted to do was provide consumers with exactly the right information, exactly when they wanted it. Now I can give them what they want, when they want it. It was very hard to do, prior to the Web."

While some con-
sumers are consumed
by the sheer joys of
product research and
bargain hunting, true
consumer confidence

FOR RETAILERS THE WEB DID NOT REVOLUTIONIZE OUR THINKING. IT REVOLUTIONIZED OUR DELIVERY.

Dan Finkelman, The Limited, Inc.

comes not from paying the lowest possible price but from believing that we've gotten a good deal for what we wanted or needed. A low price may not be such a bargain if a product is used or reconditioned, or an older model; and a high price may be warranted if a product is rare, in mint condition, or includes special features worth the extra cost.

When consumers have enough information and control to identify and define the products they want, negotiate the best price, and then seal the deal with confidence, they walk away feeling that they have made the right choice.

Of course if a purchase is made sight-unseen, the consumer may be a bit wary until the product shows up as promised. If it doesn't, then all bets are off, and the consumer feels taken for a ride. It's a trust-buster not only because a promise wasn't kept, but also because the control the consumer thought she or he had was in fact a mirage. And that leaves a bad taste in anybody's mouth.

That's why what happens at the point of sale and afterwards is equally important to a customer's sense of command over the process. Self-service technologies, from pay-at-the-pump in gas stations to self-checkout at the grocery store, are the ultimate in everyday consumer-controlled experiences. And for those who appreciate them and have learned to overcome the initial learning curve associated with a new process, there's no going back.

✳ THE VOICE OF THE CUSTOMER
AUTOMATE.

People are great, but not for everything. When I know what I want, or what I need, I don't necessarily need to talk to someone. I want to help myself. With the touch of a keypad, click of a mouse, or even the sound of my voice, I want to make things happen. The first time I ordered tickets online at Southwest Airlines, I was blown away by how much control I had over the whole process. And I love being able to get cash at ATMs anywhere, anytime. It reassures me that I have control of my money, day or night.

> WITH THE FLOOD OF SELF-SERVICE TECHNOLOGY COMES THE NATURAL EBB OF PERSONAL SERVICE.

But most of these do-it-yourself systems come at the price of human interaction. We may be able to check out faster, or pump-and-go, but we're also no longer chewing the fat with the guy who's fixed our car all those years while he checks our oil. With the flood of self-service technology comes the natural ebb of personal service. For some people, that's a reasonable trade-off. For those who prefer more, not less, human interaction, it may not be as valuable. Giving customers what they want, whether it's personalized service or anonymous self-service tools, is a sure way to help them feel empowered and in charge.

And therein lies the rub for consumers and companies alike: True control means having as little—or as much—help and contact as the customer wants. Hannelore Schmidt, Director of Consumer Delight and Loyalty for the online cosmetics company Reflect.com, which specializes in customized products for customers, says her company always knows who's in charge when it comes to interaction: the customers. "They really have total control over the experience," she says. "They choose whether they want to receive email

CONSUMERS HAVE TOTAL CONTROL OF HOW MUCH OR HOW LITTLE THEY WANT TO INTERACT WITH ANY SITE.

Hannelore Schmidt, Reflect.com

from us. They choose whether they want to interact with our site. They choose how much interaction they want to have. It's the way our site is, but it's also the beauty of the Internet—consumers have total control of how much or how little they want to interact with any site."

Giving customers greater control over the amounts and kinds of interactions and contacts they have with a company is indeed one of the benefits of the Web. But companies can give consumers greater control over these issues even when they're off-line. Because the balance of control has shifted, companies have to view their customer connections as a dialogue instead of a monologue (or a megaphone announcement). Communications are two-way these days, as consumers tell companies how and when they want to be contacted. Direct-marketing standbys, such as mail drops and telemarketing (and newer variations, such as mass email campaigns), are losing their effectiveness with consumers who are weary of junk mail and calls.

Companies are taking a cue and learning to restrain themselves from constant communications with consumers who haven't requested that level of contact. Smarter still: Companies can take a consumer-empowerment stance by assisting consumers who have asked for reduced contact by educating them about how to add their names to state or national "Do Not Call" (DNC) lists, and how to sign up with services such as JunkBusters, which help consumers staunch the flow of unwanted communications.

✳ THE VOICE OF THE CUSTOMER
DON'T CALL ME, I'LL CALL YOU.

You say we have a relationship—so why does it feel so one-sided? I give you my money and my contact information . . . and then what? You start calling, mailing, and spamming me as if we're life-long friends? If we're in this together that means I need a voice, and you need to listen when I tell you how and when you can get in touch. When you respect me by letting me control our communications, we both have something to gain.

Here's how to keep me on the line . . .

- **Not so fast.** Okay, I've given you my contact information. But hold on a sec—there are limitations. I want to weigh in on how, and how frequently, you contact me. I recently called American Express to activate a new card, and they asked my permission before sending out a "welcome" email. Nice touch! You see, maybe I just want email alerts and news. And only monthly, unless I've indicated other-wise. Maybe I want you to call me only for appointment reminders or service delays. And when it comes to cata-logs, I may want them all the time, or just quarterly, or only before the holidays. So let me define how and when you reach out and touch me. Then, when you do, I'll be happy to hear from you.

- **Slice the spam.** You just can't help yourself, can you?! Despite my specific requests, it seems you have some-thing you have to say. You call me, or more likely, you send an unsolicited email. Sure—for you, it's easy, fast, and cheap. But on my end it's piling up in my already overstuffed email box. I won't have time to read it, let alone react to it, and pretty soon I'll just filter you out even if you're sending me something I might otherwise want to read. So think twice before you hit "Send," and resist the urge to wear out your welcome.

Consumers are becoming aware of the fact that almost every purchase, every transaction, every newsletter or email list or membership they sign up for is a vehicle for gathering data into a growing mountain of personal information about them. Being able to stay in command of the how, where, why, and what of a company's information use is another critical piece of the control pie for consumers.

Recent changes in U.S. consumer protection laws and privacy policies have forced companies to disclose their practices and to give consumers more effective ways of removing their names from databases and mailing lists. But in Europe these kinds of protections are nothing new—in fact, consumers in European Union nations routinely have the option of accessing, deleting, updating, or otherwise changing any information that's been collected about them.

But whether or not the law demands it, any company that wants to gain their customers' trust by giving them control needs to make a good-faith effort to help their customers manage the information collected about them. In a best-case scenario that would mean customers could simply wipe the slate clean, if they didn't want to have their information stored, merged, and shared for future reference and marketing. Since consumer data is becoming such a valuable commodity—some companies make more money on the sale of their customer information than on the products they sell to those customers—it's unlikely that businesses will willingly relinquish their hold on their customers' data.

✳ TOWARD A MORE PRIVATE EUROPE: PRIVACY LAWS KEEP CONSUMERS IN CONTROL

Marketing to consumers based on the information that they themselves have provided—who they are, what they buy, and how they live—is as American as apple pie and baseball. But don't say that to Europeans, who view any and all private information as strictly personal.

And with good reason: Europe has a long and often ugly history of its peoples' information being used against them. One only has to think back to the Spanish Inquisition or the Holocaust, to get to times when citizens were brutalized owing to their backgrounds or beliefs. But even in the comparatively innocuous world of online commerce, Europeans have held firm to the highest standards of information privacy.

The European Commission Directive on Data Protection, enacted in 1998 by the European Union (EU), guaranteed consumers the right to complete control over their information; and as of July 2001, any company anywhere—including in the United States—can be criminally prosecuted for breaking those rules.

So what's an American company that's used to collecting, mining, and crunching consumer information to do, as it tries to move into the global marketplace? The Clinton Administration negotiated a plan with the EU known as "Safe Harbor," whereby companies can continue doing business in Europe if they agree to—and can prove their adherence to—seven principles designed to protect European citizens' right to data privacy.

Here are the seven Safe Harbor principles:

1. **Notice.** Companies must notify consumers about the purposes of the information collection, including how their information will be used.

2. **Choice.** Consumers must have the choice to "opt out" of having their information shared with a third party, or used for any purpose other than that for which the information was originally collected.

3. **Onward transfer (transfers to third parties).** Companies must apply the first two principles (Notice and Choice) to any third-party transfer of consumer information.

4. **Access.** Consumers must have the right to access, correct, or delete information that has been collected about them.

5. **Security.** Companies must take reasonable precautions to protect collected consumer information from unauthorized access, fraud, or other misuses or abuses.

6. **Data integrity.** Companies must collect and use personal information only for relevant reasons, and should ensure that this information is accurate, complete, and up-to-date.

7. **Enforcement.** Companies must provide consumers with easy and affordable mechanisms for taking independent action, if they feel their rights have been denied; must implement procedures for verifying their Safe Harbor compliance; and must remedy consumer problems brought about by compliance failures.

Will American consumers ever gain similar legal rights? The Consumer Privacy Protection Act (H.R. 2135), introduced into the U.S. House of Representatives in June 2001, was designed to offer American consumers many of the same protections afforded Europeans. By the end of 2001, however, no real action had been taken, and Congress had shifted its focus to issues other than consumer privacy rights.

But why should companies wait for legislation to force the issue? The principles of Safe Harbor are good, sound business practices that should be adapted by any company seeking to earn the trust and loyalty of its consumers. Smart companies will apply Safe Harbor not only to their European operations but also to all operations, including those in the United States. Why not take the lead by giving consumers access and control over their information now, thereby setting the standards for others to follow?

THE VOICE OF THE CUSTOMER
LET ME CONTROL MY INFORMATION.

I know you collect all sorts of stuff about me. Since I shop a lot with credit cards and often fill out membership questionnaires, I suspect you've got a nice thick file on me. But what do you know exactly? What I buy? How much I spend, where, and how often? And what are you *doing* with my info? Do you discuss it in a big fancy boardroom, or leave it sitting in an insecure computer somewhere? Are you selling it to the highest bidder? This is the stuff, frankly, that freaks me out! I'd feel a lot better if you'd let me stay in control of my info, even after you've collected it.

Let me clue you in on what matters to me here . . .

■ **Open up.** Show me everything you've got on me, and let me review it, correct it, delete it, or update it anytime I want. I've learned the hard way that credit reports can hurt me if they are inaccurate; and left unattended, small errors tend to snowball into big problems for me. Even if I opted in or willingly shared info with you, I still should have the right to change my preferences and update my account information.

■ **I want a say in how my info is shared.** My personal information isn't meant for the world. That's why it's personal. If I chose to entrust it to you, it's only reasonable that I have some say about who you give, share, or sell my info to. I want to know all the companies who may get my information from you, and then I want to have a chance to decide whether or not they should have access to my files. So you'd better be thinking about me and my needs when you sign a deal with another company, because I'll be watching closely.

■ **Don't punish me if I don't feel like sharing.** Will you please resist the urge to hold it against me if I've decided not to share my info, or if I've prohibited you from selling it to someone else? Maybe I've simply told you never to call me or send me an email. If so, please respect my desire to be left alone, and don't treat me like a second-class citizen, or deny me good prices or helpful customer service, just because I'm not playing by your rules.

COMPANIES HAVE TO VIEW THEIR CUSTOMER CONNECTIONS AS A DIALOGUE INSTEAD OF A MONOLOGUE.

Loosening the grip even just a bit can go a long way. Allowing customers to view their account information at will, and to delete wrong information or otherwise correct inaccuracies, is smart business in many ways, not the least of which is the savings in data cleansing that can be realized when customers keep their own data tidy. Going a step further, and allowing customers to identify which kinds of information they want kept private (such as purchase histories or personal preferences), also gives them a sense that they can maintain a modicum of control over what the world knows about them. Giving customers the option of shopping anonymously is another way of empowering them to stay in command of their data from the beginning.

On the flip side, companies that really want to collect and sell their customer data should consider using incentives to reward customers for providing the raw material they need to fill their data mines. Whether we're talking about membership points, special sales, or other promotional benefits, customers will feel more in command of the situation when they know they're getting some sort of value back in exchange for their information. It feels more like a two-way street, if both parties are getting something out of it.

THE VOICE OF THE CUSTOMER
LET ME BE ANONYMOUS.

You don't know me today because I don't want you to. Maybe I'm paying cash. Or maybe I'm simply not signing in to my membership area before shopping online with you. Either way, I'd really rather keep to myself, thank you very much. If I want to tell you who I am, I will. But please remember, if you want to keep my business, that sometimes it's none of yours who I am or what I'm buying.

Some companies may find it tough to just let go by giving their customers more say in what they buy, how they buy it, and what happens to their information or the relationship once the deal is done. But really this is no tougher than learning to have a real relationship with another person—getting back what you put into that relationship means letting your friend or partner take the wheel sometimes, and then just sitting back and enjoying the ride.

Putting customers in charge really means giving people what they want, when they want it, and how they want it. Whether dressed up or dressed down, mechanized or personalized, service with a smile or service with a self-scanner, control is in the eye of the beholder.

DEMANDMENT 04: **PUT ME IN CHARGE—SELF-EVALUATION**

Now that you've read this Demandment, see how you stack up. The checkpoints in this form reflect the key takeaways from the "Voice of the Customer" sections. Identify where your company could stand some improvement, and you'll have a shot at building bridges with the people who keep you in business.

4. PUT ME IN CHARGE	Excellent	Good	Poor
Get out of my way!	Provide an empowering comprehensive, self-service experience.	Consumers can transact with company with minimal assistance.	Consumers cannot transact with. company without assistance.
Don't trap me.	Let consumers make their own path, with clear access to all exits.	Let consumers make their own path.	Consumers are led down a path not necessarily of their choosing.
Automate.	Use automated processes, to ensure greater control and speed at the point of sale.	Use automated processes to ensure greater control.	Automated processes are not utilized to improve control and speed.
Don't call me, I'll call you.	Consumers decide how, and how often, to hear from company.	Consumers decide how they want to hear from company.	Consumers have no control over communications from company.
Let me control my information.	Consumers can edit their info and dictate how it's shared.	Consumers can update their information and opt in and out of sharing policies.	Consumers have no access to their information.
Let me be anonymous.	Consumers can have the option to shop as a guest.	Consumers aren't automatically registered when they make a purchase.	Consumers must register or otherwise identify themselves when making a purchase.

05

The Fifth Demandment

guide me

THE WORLD IS CONFUSING ENOUGH these days, and even when we're standing still, we often feel the need for a compass, a map, or at least some good signposts to help us get moving, see what's up ahead, and understand where we're going. Sometimes we even need a tow, to pull us out of a rut and get us back on the road again.

Like any good local tour guide, shepherding travelers through a new place of interest, a company or service provider that educates, interprets, and points out the key features along the way is empowering its consumers to take informed control of their decisions. This guidance may come in the form of a full product demonstration (the scenic tour), a helping hand out of a decision ditch, or just some directions about where to turn at a crossroads.

No matter the method or the level of help, companies that share their knowledge show their consumers that they know what they're doing and are there to help them, every step of the way and every mile of the journey. And by arming consumers with the resources they need to make smart selections, by helping them to gain confidence through knowledge, and by steering them past the pitfalls of the process, companies prove themselves to be trustworthy and trusted authorities.

The Fourth Demandment—**Put Me in Charge**—is about handing over the keys and putting consumers in the driver's seat. But that doesn't mean they want to take this journey alone. In fact they may even need a little help, starting the engine and getting on the road. And though they may not admit it they might even require a few driving lessons, or at least some navigation tips to keep them from getting lost.

So pull out that instructor's manual, unfold your roadmap, and get ready to roll, because the Fifth Demandment—**Guide Me**—is about riding alongside consumers and guiding them through the gridlock, over the speed-bumps, and around the most dangerous curves, on their way to getting exactly what they want and need.

Consumers expect that a company will know its business inside and out, and even if the consumer walks in the door armed with a library's worth of research, he or she anticipates that the salespeople or advisors will share their expertise and help him or her filter out the noise that comes along with independent research. Quite simply, while consumers demand control over the process, they're still very much in need of guided assistance, reassurance, and support when it comes to making decisions, especially about things that will significantly affect their lives, such as big-ticket purchases, real estate, health care, or insurance.

THE VOICE OF THE CUSTOMER
BOOST MY CONFIDENCE.

> I don't like to admit it, but often I get stuck when making some important buying decisions. I'm afraid I'm going to make the wrong choice; spend too much money—or not enough; pick the wrong brand. And I don't want to regret it later. Help me feel confident, whether I'm just getting started and looking for information or at a crossroads, torn between two options. Help me make good decisions and we'll both be happy.

Guidance is about demystification, training, and knowledge transfer; it passes along your expertise to consumers, who then walk away with a real understanding of what they're getting and getting themselves into, provided to them by the folks who know this stuff better than they do. And with that understanding comes the empowerment that consumers need, to close the deal without misgivings.

Consumers welcome good advice and helpful guidance from people who understand the difference between shoving and showing. Giving as much or as little help as a consumer needs may require a bit of intuition, but smart companies know how to permeate their experiences with meaningful decision support and how to train expert-yet-friendly people to help consumers in whatever way they may need assistance or aid.

> THERE'S A RISK FOR ANY BRAND THAT TRIES TO BECOME MORE A PART OF PEOPLE'S LIVES THAN IT HAS A RIGHT TO BE.
>
> **Brian McNamara,**
> **Proctor & Gamble**

Brand egotism, however, sometimes can get in the way of relevant assistance. Brian McNamara, Brand Manager for Procter & Gamble's Tide, says it's important for a brand to always understand its place in the world, and never to overstep its bounds in the lives of consumers. "What it comes down to is, we're a laundry detergent," he says. "We aren't going to solve world peace. So that's a context that we all have. It is in the context of who we are. I think there's a risk for any brand that tries to become more a part of people's lives than it has a right to be."

Keeping that relevance caveat in mind, it still is true that there's nothing quite like a well-trained and knowledgeable consultant or customer service representative, to help a consumer clear the decision-hurdles that can lead to a sale. The human factor is still critical, despite all our technology, because people relate to other people, plain and simple. And when a brand needs to relate to people at the most relevant and appropriate level, there's nothing quite like a warm voice and a helping hand.

True, we do rely on technology to deliver the background information that supports our decisions. But it's the combination of the personal touch and the richness of information technology that transforms the decision-making process into a learning process. And ultimately this process can bond the expert and the novice together, as knowledge flows from the company to the consumer and as trust flows back in the other direction, from the consumer to the company.

The most powerful people in the higher-stakes decision chain used to be three-piece-suited professionals—bankers, insurance agents, and investment brokers, to name a few—who sat at heavy oak desks projecting an air of fail-safe wisdom. Consumers once relied on them for the final word on what they should buy or do, and trustingly signed on the bottom line, assuming that these guys (and they were almost always guys) knew best.

But authoritarian figures don't quite cut it anymore—people need and want good advice that they feel comes from someone who knows their world, life, and needs as a good friend might. People still turn to professionals to open a dialogue, offer advice and perspective, and streamline the paperwork; but many consumers now also want to possess richer, deeper, and more meaningful information before they make a decision that will affect their lives.

Today's bankers, brokers, lawyers, and even doctors must also be educators and guidance counselors, helping people to understand the implications of their decisions and providing them with the resources or referrals they need to make informed choices.

But it doesn't take an office suite to make an advisor. The people we encounter behind the counter in everyday life have long shaped our

IT DOESN'T TAKE AN OFFICE SUITE TO MAKE AN ADVISOR.

decisions. From the butcher or the baker to the florist or the video-store clerk, we rely on the knowledge of people whose business it is to know more about the products they sell than we do. It helps that they've learned our tastes and preferences over the years; if not, they'll probably engage in a bit of chatty needs-assessment to find out what we're looking for before they make a suggestion.

Whether we turn to the restaurant sommelier to help us pick the perfect wine, or seek suggestions on a pair of shoes from a retail store associate, we expect that the recommendations offered us will be based not on a desire to push a particular product, but rather on the experts' own honest opinions.

So when a waiter recommends the soup of the day and it's fabulous, we know on our next visit that we can trust his opinion, and we'll listen closely to his recommendations. But if that soup ends up tasting like yesterday's dishwater, we'll assume he was just helping the chef get rid of the dregs in the pot, and we may not be back again.

Great customer-service associates and salespeople are trained to do the right thing right from the start: After all, it's their job to give people the information they need in the most relevant and absorbable way possible. But to give today's consumers the level of support they expect and demand, companies need to develop a killer combination of deep, intimate knowledge and meaningful decision assistance. And it's got to be served up on a genuine human level, without the dishwater flavor.

✳ THE VOICE OF THE CUSTOMER
KNOW YOUR STUFF.

When you have an intimate knowledge of what you're selling, and share it with me in a passionate, helpful way, I'm interested. Your confidence becomes my desire. I love it when a waiter can articulately describe each entrée, including its preparation and ingredients; and it's even better if he can

> make a heartfelt personal recommendation based on what
> he actually likes on the menu. It's hard to resist that sort of
> tip from someone in the know. If you're both proud and sin-
> cere about what you have to offer, I'll give it a try.

It's not that people need to have their hands held by sales associates, or be spoon-fed information to make a decision—after all, from the Internet to the "Dummies" guides, the wealth of information available on almost any topic can be tapped like a fire hose to transform novices into know-it-alls in no time flat. And no matter how much information a brand or company provides, consumers still may seek additional, independent opinions, reviews, and suggestions from industry-media and nonpartisan sources such as *Consumer Reports.* But by offering a bit of guidance in a world of information overload, companies show their customers that they care enough to help them get the most out of their purchase even after the money has changed hands.

The Syms Corp. may not be a household name, but this respected Mid-Atlantic-region clothing discounter has long proclaimed that "An educated

AN EDUCATED CONSUMER IS OUR BEST CUSTOMER.

Syms Corp

consumer is our best customer." Syms, which opened its first store in New York City in 1939, has lived up to that promise over the decades by color-coding its sizing tags (for easier rack-spotting by customers), dating its markdowns (so customers can see how long a piece had been on the sales floor), and posting its store policies in easy view of customers (so everyone knows the score on sales and returns). Sure, these are simple, basic ways of keeping people informed—but such essential dedication to guidance has earned Syms two generations of educated consumers and best customers.

In an era where commercial products are our chosen tools for tackling virtually every chore and fulfilling almost any need, it seems only natural that consumers will look to the companies that developed these products for related advice. Thus brands are wisely capitalizing on this growing consumer expectation and reliance on their knowledge to put together consumer education efforts that build trust. It's a new kind of soft sell that works best when companies stand beside their consumers, offering coaching and guidance rather than pitches and persuasion. Let's call this gentler model "shoulder-to-shoulder selling."

Shoulder-to-shoulder selling is not about pushing or pulling, it's about sharing and showing. It's about helping people to get the most out of products or services by giving them a greater understanding of how to choose them and use them. Visit a Gateway Country store and you'll find stations of computers to sit down at and try out, and knowledgeable salespeople who can walk you through the paces of each machine. Or step into a Sephora store and ask anyone on staff to help—they'll give you a free makeup consultation, decipher the aisles of cosmetics for you, and help you find the right brands and products for your needs. What won't they do? Intimidate you with an array of products displayed in museum-quality glass cases, or pressure you to buy a multistep beauty regimen that requires an instruction manual when all you're looking for is a good daily moisturizer.

Sephora also offers a rich consultative experience online, with "Ask the Expert" areas that provide insights from professional makeup artists and dermatologists. And they're not alone in offering online advice. Most companies got wise to the Web's informational capabilities a few years ago, and now you'd be hard-pressed to find any major brand that lacks a Web site as part of its suite of consumer communications. The beauty of the Web is that it can offer

✳ AS THE TIDE TURNS: A NEW BRAND OF AUTHORITY

When you've got a tough stain to conquer, who are you gonna turn to for advice: a no-name Web site, or your old pal Tide? Back in 1996, Procter & Gamble gambled that consumers would prefer a nonbranded laundry-authority when exploring the still relatively commercial-free zone of the Web, and so clothesline.com was born.

But P&G market research revealed a surprising trend: Consumers were scouring the Web for a site from Tide, looking to the stalwart laundry-detergent brand as a more reliable ally in their war against stains.

By 2000, P&G had decided to come clean, spinning the content and features of its clothesline.com site into the bubbly and heavily branded Tide.com site, complete with such tools as The Stain Detective, which offers tips on getting out any stain on any fabric.

In a world where companies face an uphill battle as they seek to gain the loyalty of an increasingly cynical consumer audience, hardened by brand overkill, the P&G story sounds almost like a fairytale. But it's a true story, and in large part that's because Tide and its parent company have long been focused on learning about and understanding consumers' needs, and reflecting these in their products and marketing.

So for Tide's consumers to see the laundry detergent as an authority in cleaning—a true "household" name, as it were—is far from surprising. And the company is using its technology not just to advertise the product, but to spread its message in new and meaningful ways. "The Web site has provided us with an opportunity to develop a personal connection with our consumers," says Brian McNamara, Tide's brand manager. "On a brand like Tide we communicate our message through mass media, but it is important to us to also to take the personal approach. Tide is a brand that helps people solve the problems of everyday stains and spills, and we needed a way to be able to communicate this one-on-one. That's where the Internet has been a really terrific tool, because we can offer helpful hints and tips and fabric care information, personalized to an individual's needs."

McNamara says that, true to P&G's reputation for staying ahead of the curve in understanding consumer needs, "The Internet has also provided a means through which we can stay relevant to our consumers . . . by constantly innovating through technology as well as through marketing. Being the biggest brand [of laundry detergent], we are in front of the consumer more than anyone else, but we need to do that in ways that are new and different."

Procter & Gamble's strong commitment to both consumer needs and technological innovations has led consumers to view the Web sites of Tide and other Procter & Gamble brand stars such as Noxema, Charmin, Folger's and Pepto-Bismol as richly informative and reliable sources for advice about life's everyday triumphs and tribulations.

With too many unknown or anonymous preachers and teachers offering questionable expertise, the names consumers know are also the names they turn to in their times of need—as when Junior spills chocolate syrup all over his big sister's prom dress, an hour before her date arrives.

multifaceted layers of content to support consumer decisions, doing so through everything from sample book chapters and music tracks to online tutorials, glossaries, Frequently Asked Questions (FAQs), policy summaries, and other information.

THE VOICE OF THE CUSTOMER
SIT DOWN NEXT TO ME.

You're the expert in your business. You know you best. And I'm the expert on me—I know me best! So please stop talking, shouting, or persuading, at least long enough to just sit down next to me for a few minutes. Let's go at this side-by-side, so you can help me figure this out. Because I want to trust you, and because I believe you can help me, I need to have that comfort level that comes with genuine guidance. Lose the suave salesmanship and know-it-all attitude, and we'll get along just fine.

Here are some hints for getting real with me . . .

- **Begin the dialogue.** Talk to me, prompt me, reach out, pose a question, or acknowledge my inquiry. Nothing fancy. Just friendly. I need to feel important enough for you to take me by the hand, so to speak. Look me in the eye at your service counter or reception desk, be happy to take my call, and let me know you're eager to help.

- **Listen.** Really listen! I need to know that you're really hearing what I'm saying, not just waiting for your turn to speak. From my perspective, it's all about me. So don't just follow a canned script; show you get what I've told you by reacting to my real needs and by asking the right questions. When I go to a Best Buy, for instance, I know I won't be pressured by salespeople the minute I walk in the door; but when I need someone to help me, I can always find an expert who really knows how to help me find what I'm looking for—and that's because they listen to me!

Companies that need to feed an ongoing stream of information to consumers—such as car-makers communicating about maintenance tips or recall notices—can use the Web to pour this information into personalized pages set up by the owner. Honda, Mercedes, Ford, and other car companies have rolled out just such Web-based owner pages, giving car buyers a place to access everything from repair records to virtual owner's manuals, all without rummaging through the glove compartment.

The ideal **Guide Me** experience embraces all channels, all the time. Companies such as Victoria's Secret, Target, Avon, Sears, and Barnes and Noble prove that the Web can help both companies and their consumers to complete and enrich holistic brand experiences. These companies don't treat their Web sites like stand-alone channels or communications vehicles but rather like integrated parts of the total brand experience, guiding consumers through their product lines and supporting their purchase decisions made in any and every channel.

"Our job is creating a seamless organization," explains Dan Finkelman, Senior Vice President for Brand and Business Planning for The Limited, Inc. He ought to know: The Limited, Inc. operates multiple channels for multiple brands.

Finkelman says that to get all of these pieces and parts working in unison so as to deliver to customers the information, services, and support they need, an organization must foster a cross-channel culture to bring about that holistic experience. This, he says, is the only way for a company to present a cohesive, multichannel face to its consumers. "You first have to create basically integrated, aligned parts. Literally. Or you'll never get to that external customer touch point that is seamless. In fact, today, I'd argue that for most companies it's probably more seamless to the customer than it is internally."

The information in every channel may not be identical in its context or delivery, but it's always relevant to the category, the brand, the audience, and the experience. No disconnects, no matter the channel. So when you visit bn.com, the online version of Barnes and Noble, you'll find content from *Book* magazine, with author interviews and other reports from the literary scene, as well as a free, searchable version of the *Reader's Catalog,* with associated book recommendations. Visit a Barnes and Noble store and you'll find in-store author readings and book club meetings, along with well-read sales associates who double as literary guides for their customers. In a cozy personal touch, the sales associates provide descriptions of their favorite books on hand-written cards displayed on the store shelves.

Then again, book buying is as much of a pleasure as it is a chore for most people; that means that the aesthetics of guidance in this category are far different from, say, assisting someone who's struggling to build a deck, or racing the clock to decorate a nursery. When it comes to decision-support heavy lifting, one of the best facilitators is Home Depot, which thinks of its stores and its Web site as opportunities to teach and to guide consumers through the maze of home-improvement products and projects.

Anyone who's visited a Home Depot store knows they'll find an expert equipped with good advice and recommendations for almost any task, large or small. And the Web site—which, granted, usually

✳ HOME DEPOT: HANDYMAN'S SPECIALS

Home improvement is one of those unavoidable consequences of life, like death and taxes. For some people it's a burden, for others a joy—and for millions, it's a bit of both. That's why superstars of the sawhorse set, like Bob Villa, have developed such a following, and why the long-running Tim Allen sitcom, *Home Improvement,* was so endearingly on target.

With American home ownership having risen steadily ever since World War II, it was only to be expected that a company like Home Depot would come along to transform the old-fashioned hardware store into a do-it-yourself destination on a grand scale. Since its founding in Atlanta in 1978, Home Depot has risen to the top of the woodpile not simply by being the biggest of the big-box hardware stores but, more importantly, by offering help and guidance in every conceivable form.

With its online do-it-yourself training and its in-home installation, its trained associates who can talk not just to contractors but like contractors, and its culture based on the importance of customer empowerment, Home Depot has taken the do-it-yourself world to a whole new level.

No wonder it made *Fortune* magazine's list of the top ten most admired companies in 2001, or that for a decade it has ranked at that top of the magazine's list of specialty retailers. Simply put, Home Depot nails the idea that selling is more than just merchandising and pricing—it's also about teaching and training. From the classes customers can take in everything from how to seed their lawns to how to build their decks, to the customized planning services they can receive from trained experts, Home Depot has become a business seemingly without much room left for improvement. With more than 1500 stores across North America and into South America, this publicly traded retailer chain rakes in some $46 billion in sales annually.

However, such aggressive growth hasn't come without a price-tag, though; flattening sales, and market saturation. That's why, in 2001, the firm brought in an outside Mr. Fix-It—former General Electric executive Bob Nardelli—as CEO. Nardelli promptly rolled up his sleeves and began tightening bolts, applying elbow grease to squeaky wheels, and generally sweeping the place clean like any good contractor after a hard day's work.

What with its smart management and its consumer-centric point of view, Home Depot is sure to remain a company that knows how to get the job done by helping its customers hammer away at their home-improvement projects.

doesn't stock nearly as much stuff as the actual stores do—takes this educational strategy one better, with tutorials and tips on everything from hanging wallpaper to building decks.

The Web is clearly here to stay, as an influence in consumer buying decisions. According to the NPD Group and Jupiter Media Metrix, Inc., as of July 2001 about 97 percent of consumers with access to the Internet had used it for research purchases; of those who did their research online, 51 percent said they made their actual purchases off-line.

What with consumers having so many sources of information available to them and so many products from which to choose, knowledge-needs to support a confident purchase can spiral upward depending on how expensive, complex, or important the buying decision. Thus companies need to think carefully about how all that information they're putting out there is being used, and tier it in ways that lead consumers down a meaningful learning path by giving them relevant kinds of information at each stage of the journey toward a purchase.

THE VOICE OF THE CUSTOMER
POINT ME IN THE RIGHT DIRECTION.

Which way? How far? Are we there yet? There are so many paths for almost every choice I need to make, each with its own consequences. So I'm turning to you to help me find my way. You're the magic compass—once you know where I want to go, you can point me in the right direction. I'm not even talking about travel, specifically, though it certainly applies there too. I'm talking about the journeys of everyday life. Should I go with natural or synthetic wood for the kitchen floor? How can I find the right pediatrician for my child? And will any of those toothpastes *really* whiten my teeth? Those are some the questions rattling through my head. Answer them for me, and I'll be all ears!

Here's a guide to being my guide. . . .

■ **Educate me.** Share with me what you know. I want to learn, absorb, soak it all in. Give me the what, why, and how of what I need to understand, and do it in an interesting way. The more I learn, the more committed I become to you, your products, brands, ideas, activities, and events. Thanks to helpful companies I've recently learned how to buy a diamond (Tiffany's had all the answers for me) and how to get out a catsup stain (thank you, Tide.com's Stain Detective!). When you're a good teacher with the right message, I'll be a good student and a good customer.

■ **Seeing is believing.** I have trouble visualizing. I like to touch and feel, or ideally see, your products in action. Will they work, fit, do the trick? That's why, admittedly, I sometimes get sucked into QVC when I'm channel-surfing. And now they even have Outlet Centers in some resort cities, where people can interact first-hand with what they're selling.

■ **Let me learn from others, too.** Sometimes you have to step aside. Make way for others. I'm not out to make new friends, but I do want to learn from other people to whom I can relate. Not necessarily professionals with multiple degrees, but ordinary people who have had experiences I can learn from. So help me connect with, say, couples that conquered infertility; cancer survivors; stock market winners; travel buffs; real estate gurus; food fanatics; book lovers; and so on. I really love the Genius Bar at my local Apple Store—it gives geeks like me a place to hang out and chat about bits and bytes, when I stop by to check out the latest gadgets.

We've come to expect that, wherever we turn, information will flow at us to help us understand what we need to know or what we should do next. It may not be well designed or neatly delivered, but we still expect it to be there. We may even take it for granted that our cereal boxes will have nutritional labeling; that our prescription bottles will come with patient-information inserts; and that our new cars will be equipped not only with airbags but also with warning stickers to tell us how to avoid being injured by them.

In all of those cases we can thank Uncle Sam, for consumer-protection regulations that mandate labeling and information on many of the products and much of the packaging we encounter daily. The U.S. government insists that a lot of this kind of information be disclosed to consumers by way of regulations covering everything from airlines and banks to food-makers and pharmaceutical manufacturers. The government also disseminates plenty of free consumer info: The Federal Consumer Information Center (FCIC) Web site—www.pueblo.gsa.gov—offers a vast array of downloadable publications containing tips on everything from how to buy a used car to how to eat right for healthy teeth.

Though many companies comply with government regulations through fine-print disclosures, to win lasting customer loyalty they need to go beyond the letter of the law by reacting to their customers' needs, not just the requirements of federal mandates. By going that extra mile and making consumer information even easier to find and take away (say, in helpful hand-outs or printable PDFs), to read (with larger print and better graphical layout), and to use (such as "how-to" guides that teach customers something worth learning), companies can go a long way toward earning the gratitude and trust of their customers.

✳ THE VOICE OF THE CUSTOMER
FILTER THE NOISE.

There's a lot of info-noise out there, and it's making me crazy. Everybody is selling me something, from celebrity talking heads on cable TV to stacks of junk mail and screens full of email spam, and they're all making product-promises and service-claims I don't have the time or the energy to investigate. So listen up: If you want my time and attention, start making sense.

Ready to help me cut through the clutter? Here are some tips . . .

- **Organize the chaos.** You have a lot to say. And just maybe, I want to hear it, see it, be a part of it. But don't bombard me with everything you want to say. Begin by getting organized. Let me know what's most important by putting it front and center. The nitty-gritty details can fall away or drop to the bottom, but don't try to trick me with fine print! Just help me get the most out of what you're trying to tell me.

- **Bite size, for starters.** When I'm getting a feel for something, a little taste often is enough to whet my appetite. Sometimes a few facts or stats are all I need to make a decision, so break that stuff out into nice little nuggets for me to nibble on, first. Then, if I want to know more, make it easy for me to dig deeper.

While we may cringe at late-night infomercials, they do help people to see products in action. And that's a necessity in many cases, since the products sold are usually from smaller brands or are new inventions that consumers haven't seen anywhere before. Production values (and audiences paid to clap) aside, they give viewers an on-the-spot lesson in how to use what they're selling. For a real lesson in how to tell and sell, look no further than the QVC home shopping channel and its Internet outlet, iQVC, which supplements the on-air demonstrations and sales pitches with deeper product information, gift suggestion tools, specialty stores, and other helpful ways to engage, inform, and educate QVC customers.

Or watch such demo masters as "Body by" Jake Steinfeld sell exercise equipment, or inventor and infomercial innovator Ron Popeil sell anything from his Popeil Pocket Fisherman to his Automatic 5-minute Pasta & Sausage Maker, and you'll see the magic of demonstration in action. These guys both show *and* tell, and it works like a charm on millions of viewers who might otherwise have passed by their products on store shelves.

But it's the big-ticket or life-altering acquisitions, investments, and decisions that really tax a person's ability to make an informed choice. So when it comes to buying our first house, selecting the right college for our kids, or investing for retirement, we rely on the informed opinions of experts, on technological tools like online calculators and recommendation engines, and on the advice of peers and respected sources to help us understand the full implications of our options.

> **ENTIRE INDUSTRIES HAVE MIGRATED AWAY FROM THE HARD SELL AND THE FAST HANDSHAKE TO NEWER, SOFTER METHODS.**

Entire industries, notably banking and finance, life insurance and real estate, have migrated away from the older tactics of the hard sell and the fast handshake to the newer, softer methods of peddling their products and services by educating their customers and earning their trust (and business) in the process. With customers no longer willing simply to sign on the dotted line without first doing some deeper review and research, insurance agencies, for instance, are refocusing their sales training on helping to educate consumers by means of "life event" information. This allows families to understand the intricacies of planning in relation to everything from a new baby to an early retirement.

THE VOICE OF THE CUSTOMER
ANTICIPATE MY NEEDS.

I admit it: I'm a sucker for instant gratification. Yeah, I'm a tad embarrassed about it, but I can't help it! That's where you come in. Help me to move beyond the moment so I can also see the big picture. Look down the road with me. Will this still be the right decision for me a year or more from now? As my life changes in expected (or unexpected) ways, do you think it will be the smartest solution in the long run? Are there milestones I should know about, moments when it would be wise for me to reevaluate what I need? I may not invest in the long haul now, but at least there won't be as many surprises down the road, and I'll appreciate it later.

Here's how to help me see what's in store. . . .

■ **Get out in front.** I like to be on top of things, but keeping up in this day and age has become impossible. So give me a heads-up now and then—tip me off about things that are new, important, on sale, or otherwise relevant to my life. BabyCenter.com sent me regular emails throughout my pregnancy—they helped me to understand what I was going through, and they not only suggested products and services I could actually use but did so when I actually needed them. And now I get regular email newsletters that relate to the stages of my child's development.

- **Suggest a route, and help me stay on track.** I realize I can't have a dream home overnight. Or a perfect physique. Or a mindful child, for that matter. But I can take small steps toward each or all of those goals, if you help me. Create a plan for me. Give me step-by-step instructions for getting from here to there. A roadmap for my life, of sorts. And show me where I'm likely to run into slow-downs, delays, barriers, or other hardships that may make for a bumpy ride—and give me alternate routes to help me avoid them. Then let me track my progress, so I feel good about myself as I get closer to my destination.

- **Let me keep a copy.** There is nothing worse than first gazing into the crystal ball with you and getting seduced by a grand plan, only to then be left empty-handed. Give me a copy. Or keep a file that I can access. I'll go back to it from time to time, to monitor my progress, make adjustments, or ask for additional guidance.

Healthcare/medicine is probably the leading area that elicits consumer interest in information and guidance, both virtual and real. When faced with an illness, a medical condition, or procedure, patients and their loved ones no longer settle for a simple second opinion. They actively seek out and drill down through as many related resources as they can find, starting with friends and family and the educational materials provided by their doctor(s), but then quickly branching out into consumer and medical journals, patient-support groups, online message boards or newsgroups, pharmaceutical company consumer information, and government and private research organizations.

Healthcare companies are getting the message, now spending millions to integrate patient-information systems into their online systems and finding new ways to teach patients how to better manage their health. And it's not just about the cost savings associated with wellness check-ups as opposed to sickness appointments. With the advent of the Internet, Americans have been taking their health-information-gathering into their own hands.

Since 1998, The Harris Poll Interactive has been tracking the growing online population of what it has dubbed "cyberchondriacs"— those who use the Web for healthcare research. Over the course of only three years, the pollsters tracked an astonishing rise in the number of Americans using the Web to research medical information, from its initial 1998 count of 54 million adult researchers (about 70 percent of the entire online community at that time) to almost 100 million online researchers by April 2001 (accounting for about 75 percent of all adults online).

That's a lot of people looking up a lot of information; it's only natural that their healthcare providers should now be steering their patients toward the best and most reliable sources. Caregivers who thus guide their patients through the maze of medical information available to them are essentially training them to take charge of their own health.

Consumers are paradoxical people—they want certain things done a certain way for a certain reason—but often they need some help in understanding what those things are, how they should be done, and why. Companies that share their expertise and knowledge with consumers, to help them make smart decisions, are doing more than just selling their wares. They're enabling their consumers to feel confident and comfortable in their choices.

Guidance is perhaps the most important kind of customer support, simply because it supports not only the decision and the sale but also the evolution of a trusting and loyal relationship between a company and its customers.

DEMANDMENT 05: **GUIDE ME—SELF-EVALUATION**

Now that you've read this Demandment, see how you stack up. The checkpoints in this form reflect the key takeaways from the "Voice of the Customer" sections. Identify where your company could stand some improvement, and you'll have a shot at building bridges with the people who keep you in business.

5. GUIDE ME	Excellent	Good	Poor
Boost my confidence.	Routinely help consumers feel confident, when making important decisions.	Often help consumers feel confident when making important decisions.	Building consumer confidence is a low priority.
Know your stuff.	Passion and deep product expertise (spoken or implied) stimulates desire.	Deep product expertise influences desire.	Fail to leverage product expertise so as to influence consumer desire.
Sit down next to me.	Attentive listening and side-by-side assistance is used, in lieu of persuasive tactics.	Side-by-side assistance is used, in lieu of persuasive tactics.	Persuasion is the only form of sales.
Point me in the right direction.	Provide helpful content, tools, or advice that leads consumers through buying process.	Provided helpful content, tools, or advice.	Do not provide consumers with helpful content, tools, or advice to aid in the buying process.
Filter the noise.	Remove communication clutter and summarize relevant information.	Summarize relevant information.	Provide information in excess that is not filtered for relevance.
Anticipated my needs.	Provide consumers with relevant action plan, and tips for staying on track.	Provide consumers with relevant action plan.	Focus on selling consumers what they need today, without helping them to think about their needs of tomorrow.

06

The Sixth
Demandment

24/7

TIME IS OF THE ESSENCE, and timing is everything. Just ask anyone who's spent hours in line to buy tickets to a hot concert, only to have the show sell out just before they got to the sales window. Or anyone who's been stuck on the phone as the minutes ticked by, listening to endless loops of canned music while waiting for "the next available representative."

We live in a world where pace has overtaken precision, where news is a constant feed from cable TV and the Internet, and where people can buy or do almost anything, anytime and anywhere. It's both a timely and a time-consuming issue: The 24/7 world demands that companies find ways to fulfill their customers' needs at all times and in as many channels and outlets as possible. But businesses must fill this bottomless time-pit without endangering their brand by overextending their ability to deliver quality experiences.

WE LIVE IN A WORLD WHERE PACE HAS OVERTAKEN PRECISION

Tick, tock, tick, tock: It's time for the Sixth Demandment—**24/7**. Coming of age in the era of "Internet Time," this term for 'round-the-clock activity and access reflects a world that seems to be spinning a little faster, shrinking a little smaller, and working a little harder than it was in the days before cell phones and video-on-demand, Instant Messaging (IM), and same-day delivery.

THE UNTHINKABLE A GENERATION AGO IS NOW THE UNREMARKABLE.

For many people living busy lives, 24/7 has become a way of life. The unthinkable a generation ago is now the unremarkable, to many people who take for granted the modern conveniences born of beat-the-clock competition and the consumer-driven need for speed. A critical mass of time barriers has been broken in the past few decades—from Federal Express's overnight package delivery services to CNN's around-the-clock headline-news cablecasts to Kinko's 24-hour-a-day office service centers—and each new innovation in time-less convenience ups the ante, as consumers expect increasingly fast response and 24/7 service from companies that might once have been able to operate on a standard 9-to-5 schedule.

THE VOICE OF THE CUSTOMER
REMOVE THE WALLS.

Think of your business not as a mere place but as, say, an experience, one not bound by walls, phones, time, or even people. You have things I may want. It's just that I may not have the time to drop by when you want me to. So figure out how to be open and available for me, when I'm ready to experience what you have to offer.

Here's how to break down the walls in your thinking. . . .

■ **Redefine your idea of business hours.** Get your hours in synch with my needs: Think about when I'm going to be able to drop by or call, and then make sure you're there for me. And whatever you do, don't take your cue from car dealers, who always seem to close their lots on the only day I'm free to browse or buy! If I have to work you into my schedule, instead of the other way around, I may not even bother.

■ **Don't shut down on me.** Even if you've locked the doors and turned out the lights for the day, I should be able to get in touch with you. It doesn't matter why, really— whether I need driving directions, account information, or some additional support after I've brought something home. All you need to know is that I like to feel I can count on you for service and support—24/7.

■ **Talk around the clock.** If you claim to offer 24/7 service and support, I expect just that: Someone who is available to help me in the middle of the day or night. If this is more than you can manage, then don't make the claim. At least let me leave a message on your machine or on your site. I can be okay with that, as long as I hear back from you—within 24 hours, of course.

Demandment Three, **Make It Easy,** is all about convenience, and this Demandment takes that idea and adds the layer of always-on, always-there access. Think of convenience stores: They're convenient for two reasons—one, their hours (often open 24/7, or at least later than most stores) and two, their ubiquity (seemingly they're every-where, especially now that most gas stations have opened their own mini-marts).

In a 24/7 world, consumers are less forgiving of locked doors, busy phone lines, banker's hours, and blanket form letters or auto-responses. They expect to hear a real voice on the other line, no matter when they call; to be able to shop for cat food at four in the morning; to watch their favorite TV shows on their own schedules, not the network programmer's; and to do their banking and bill-paying from home or at the office, on the road, on vacation, and at any time of the day, night, or year.

And even if they've had months to prepare, they want to be able to do their taxes at the last minute and file them electronically, or order holiday gifts two days before Christmas and have them delivered on time. They want it all, and they want it now. Or at least, they want to know they can have it when they need it, without a wait or a worry.

A GENERATION HAS GROWN UP NOT KNOWING HOW TO GET MONEY UNLESS IT'S FROM AN ATM.

The technologies and cultures associated with a constant stream of communications, transactions, and services don't come cheap. In a society where consumers have become reliant on them, however, companies that hope to compete have more and more come to regard them as necessities. A generation has grown up not knowing how to get money unless it's from an ATM, and a horde of call-

❇ C-STORES: 'ROUND-THE-CLOCK CONVENIENCE

A study conducted at the dawn of the twenty-first century by Yankelovich Partners revealed that Americans ranked the existence of 24-hour convenience (aka "C") stores among the top three things they'd most like to see continue on into the new millennium. And with more than 120,000 locations in the United States alone, convenience stores are a trend that just keeps on growing.

Once primarily purveyors of cigarettes, candy, and coffee, convenience stores now sell everything from prepared meals to pet foods, and are undergoing a service revolution as they seek new ways to meet the needs of their busy customers. Many stores, in an effort to become true one-stop destinations, enable customers to do everything from banking at the ATM (70 percent of convenience stores now have money machines) to renting videos to dropping off dry cleaning to paying utility bills. Soon we'll probably be leaving our kids and our dogs at the local convenience store daycare center, on our way to work.

In some ways, the "C" store story is as much about opposing needs and trends as it is about changing times. For when giant, super-duper markets began to take over the role of primary grocery stores in suburban communities, suddenly the simple task of picking up a gallon of milk and a loaf of bread felt like a trek through the wilds of a consumer jungle. At the same time, pricing in convenience stores finally came into line with supermarkets, so that consumers no longer felt they were being gouged at the "C" store for the gallon of milk they had to pick up in a hurry. The convenience quotient took on even greater significance with the rise of gas-station-associated quickie marts—to the point that it's the rare block of a miracle mile or a suburban strip that lacks a string of gas station/convenience store locations.

So there you have it: Always open, always there, always easy—the "C" is here to stay for at least another century. The only thing easier would be to have your milk delivered to your back door. But that's too futuristic to even imagine, now, isn't it?

center workers—of which, according to the U.S. Department of Labor, there are more than 400,000 employed in the United States alone—routinely work the overnight shift to service the needs of off-hours customers.

But can any company really be everywhere, every way, every time, for its customers? Not easily; and not wisely, if the brand experience is endangered because quality is taking a backseat to speed. So finding the right blend of pervasiveness and perpetuity, without breaking the bank or rushing the results, is a must for today's companies and institutions.

Companies need to be able to deliver at least the appearance of having an anytime-anyplace presence. Even something as simple as having a solid knowledge base of Frequently Asked Questions (FAQs) on a Web site so that visitors can find answers whenever they need them, goes a long way toward giving people a sense that a company is "there" for them all the time.

It's not enough, though, to always be open, if your shelves aren't stocked with what your customers really need, just as it isn't enough to offer ready-made answers that aren't relevant to what your customers are asking. This idea is at the core of the next chapter, Demandment Seven—**Get to Know Me**—but it's also relevant here, because one of the keys to 24/7 success is knowing enough about your consumers to be able to serve them well at any time. Kinko's, for instance, totally gets this: Not only are their business service centers open 24/7, but they strive to know their customers' individual needs as well as to stay on top of and ahead of their needs as times and technologies change.

"With 24 x 7 service—whether at retail or on the Web—customers know that Kinko's is there when they need us," notes Charlie

---

✳ KINKO'S: THE 24/7 COPYCATS

Is it any wonder that Kinko's was founded three decades ago in a California college town? The quirkily named patron saint of all-nighters sprang to life, some three decades ago, from a simple copy shop run by a guy whose college nickname was "Kinko."

That guy, who's real name is Paul Orfalea, opened the first Kinko's in Santa Barbara, California, in September 1970. Orfalea had just graduated from the University of California, and he saw a need for a place where students and local businesspeople could stop in for some copying and perhaps a bit of offset printing as well.

While the original Kinko's featured only one photocopying machine, the demand for copies soon grew so strong that store space couldn't keep pace with the proliferation of machines. A favorite Kinko's legend tells tales of customers making copies out on the sidewalk, where machines were set up because there was no room left inside the first location.

Some three decades, and 1100 stores open around the world, later, the Kinko's story isn't so much about copies as it is about full-scale, 24/7 document services that give busy professionals and cramming students fast service and peace of mind even at four in the morning.

Charlie Morrison, Kinko's Vice President of Product Management, knows that Kinko's customers lead busy lives, which is why they depend on the company to back them up whenever and wherever they need help. "Our customers are always on the go, and almost every job is unique and on a tight turnaround," Morrison says.

And because technology has always been at the root of Kinko's success, staying on the leading edge of desktop publishing and document systems remains a critical component of the Kinko's plan. "Kinko's has always been first in our industry to deploy new technologies to customers," Morrison says. "For example, we adopted the Web and related technologies in the mid-'90s to address changes in customer needs. Today, all of our locations offer customers the choice to bring a job to us physically or online."

It's on that kind of integrated, always-on service that Kinko's has staked its claim to fame. It is all about delivering consistent quality at all hours. "The ability to electronically distribute and then print a document when customers need it, where they need it, is a unique competitive advantage for Kinko's and our customers," Morrison says. It also defines the soul of a copycat that knows how to keep a mouse busy.

Morrison, Kinko's Vice President of Product Management. "In addition, our knowledgeable team members instill confidence in our customers that their job will be done right on time. Over time, we've found that regular customers come to rely on particular team members who have helped them in the past and who know their unique needs."

Companies that span multiple channels have a natural opportunity to spread their service and support around, enough to give customers a sense of 24/7 access and assistance. Fully deployed contact centers, armed with well-trained staff and the latest technologies, can multitask for multichannels with tools that facilitate communications via telephone, email, Instant Messaging (IM), and Voice Over Internet Protocol (VOIP)—the last of which lets people talk to a customer service representative on the phone while clicking through the company's Web site.

IM, in particular, has proven to be a smart tool for keeping the communication lines open and the transactions flowing with consumers as they move on to the final buying process, when purchases often teeter precariously in the balance of oblivion owing to factors like confusing check-out processes, lack of assistance, and last-minute misgivings on the part of the consumer.

One online business that puts this technology to good use, the creative gift company UncommonGoods, provides its customers with hands-on help that can really make a difference to consumers who are trying to find just the right gift for that special person. That's not surprising, given that UncommonGoods has a culture that is uncommonly dedicated to complete customer care in all its facets.

"I view customer service as everybody's job here," says founder and CEO Dave Bolotsky. "It is one of the few areas that we have total control over and we have no excuse for screwing it up. Buying the wrong color pen is inevitable, failing to respond to a customer in a satisfactory manner is unacceptable."

I VIEW CUSTOMER SERVICE AS EVERYBODY'S JOB HERE.

**Dave Bolotsky,
UncommonGoods**

Bolotsky also says that unlike many companies that farm out their customer service duties to contact centers, the folks at UncommonGoods work the phones themselves. "We handle our fulfillment and customer service in-house, in contrast to many online retailers. And every one of our English-speaking employees has customer-service shifts. The more contact we have with the customer, the better, in my view."

According to a 2001 study by research and consulting firm Basex, e-retailers could reduce e-shopping cart abandonment by as much as 20 percent by providing an IM interface with a live customer service associate, who can provide real-time support as the consumer moves through the purchase stage.

The Basex report estimated that online stores could increase sales by up to $20 billion annually by integrating such so-called "presence services" to give consumers a sense of always-there assistance, especially at the critical moment when they click the final "Buy" button. And it makes sense: Your company wouldn't ask its consumers to move through its transaction system in a darkened room without assistance, which is why it should view the addition of IM assistance in a similar light.

Still, owing to the relatively high price of instituting IM and other constant- or instant-contact customer services, the ROI may not be easily attainable by smaller companies. But as costs shrink, companies eventually will need to install these sorts of systems to grow their business and keep up with the competition.

Land's End and Coldwater Creek both have this level of integrated contact support in play. That means that a Land's End catalog customer who decides to explore the LandsEnd.com experience will enjoy the same high level of support he's come to expect from calling the company's toll-free number—only this time, he's getting help via email and live chat when he has a question. And when a Coldwater Creek store shopper needs some last-minute holiday gifts but can't get to the mall, she can log onto the company's Web site or use its catalog—or even do both at once—to work in real time with a customer service associate who can tell her which products are available for immediate shipping and then place the order.

On-the-spot communications can make a difference in a company's ability to respond fast to customer concerns—not just while communicating directly with consumers, but also when decision makers are communicating with each other.

"Instant messenger is a great tool that we use throughout the company to make sure that questions and requests get handled ASAP," says Hannelore Schmidt, Director of Consumer Delight and Loyalty for the custom cosmetics site Reflect.com. "We have a concierge service made up of company owners. And because they are owners, they will do whatever it takes to make a customer happy. And if they cannot do it themselves, they quickly contact the appropriate person to make that happen."

As with every Demandment in this book, this sort of holistic, integrated customer-service and -support experience is both an opportunity and a challenge for companies. Done right, it strengthens consumer loyalty, extends the audience reach, and magnifies the

ONE CHANNEL'S FUMBLE MAY EVENTUALLY LEAD TO A DOMINO EFFECT IN LOYALTY IF LEFT UNRESOLVED.

brand's impact owing to its accessibility and its consistency of experience. Done poorly, though, one channel's fumble may eventually lead to a domino effect in loyalty if it is left unresolved, with faith being toppled first in the channel where the problems occurred and then eventually spreading to the brand's channels, as the consumer begins to lay the blame for the channel failure squarely at the feet of the brand itself and thus, of all of its channels.

✳ THE VOICE OF THE CUSTOMER
I NEED IT NOW!

My to-do list is never-ending. Sometimes I get a moment to tackle an errand on the way home from daycare, over lunch, during a meeting, or in the middle of the night. So I need you to be ready for me when I'm ready for you, even if that means it's at the last minute. Make my life easier by not slowing me down when I'm on the go. Give me express service. Fast service. Or self-service. Give me access in stores or online, by the phone or at the drive-through. I want options for doing business with you in whatever ways my day may demand.

Here's how to put the "now" in your how. . . .

■ **Let me drive through or drive up.** Sometimes I don't have time to take in your environment. I can't find a parking place, or don't want to wrestle my kids out of their car seats, all in the name of a quick purchase. If I was put to the test, I could subsist on everything available in drive-throughs: groceries, money, gas, beer, coffee, ice cream, and news. Let me get to you in my car, and you're likely to be routed into my routine.

- **Click and go.** I've done my homework and I know what I want. And I want it ASAP. But I only have time to do this over the Web. Do I have an account with you already? Cool. Then let me just click in, click out, and get on with my day. That's what I love about Reflect.com: They've saved my shopping list from my recent orders so I can reorder fast without having to go through all the steps again.

- **Find it for me.** If you're out of stock in a store I expect that you will, at a minimum, call another location. But even that's a hassle, because often it takes numerous calls and a trip across town. I appreciate the way the Gap connects to its companywide inventory to locate an out-of-stock item in record time. They're quick to send it off (at no charge), to win the sale and a grateful customer.

Sometimes, no matter how much you try, you can't please all the people all of the time. Providing experiences that are rich in relevant communications and rapid response can be costly, but some companies have found ways to pass that cost along to their most demanding customers by simply charging more for greater access.

The tiered-service model can be effective at reducing costs in some sectors, especially those where customers require service from highly trained professionals. This is certainly the case in computer technical support. While Apple provides 90 days of free tech support, to help new buyers over the hump of installation and learning, once that three-month time is up consumers pay a fee for each call they make. And for businesses that must keep their computers running and their people working the investment often pays for itself, which is why companies such as Hewlett-Packard have well-honed and well-respected support teams who provide 'round-the-clock assistance to business customers who have paid a premium for that service.

Being able to tier these services to the actual needs of customers only works, of course, if a company understands what those needs are. Alex Sozonoff, Vice President of Customer Advocacy at Hewlett-Packard, notes that no two customers are alike, and neither are their needs. "On the one extreme you have the customer who needs all the help, all the handholding. He wants to buy a PC but has no clue where the on/off switch is. [For that kind of customer] emails have to be foolproof, and you have to give him a support number he can call if he needs to." On the other side of the spectrum, Sozonoff says, is the low-maintenance bargain hunter. "[That person says] 'Look, I only want the lowest price. And I don't need anything else. Just give me a good manual, a low price, and I'm smart enough I can do everything myself.'"

Just as some computer users require more attention than others, so too do some patients. Which is why medicine is an area where pay-for-premium access may be particularly ripe for success. As HMOs and managed-care systems turn more and more doctors' offices into assembly-line treatment centers, a new kind of ultra-personal medical service has sprung up to serve those who are willing to pay retainers for greater access to their physicians. A growing trend, especially in wealthier communities, is that of "concierge care": physicians who collect hefty fees from a small number of patients (in some cases, a single patient) in exchange for being on call for their individual medical needs.

On a less expensive but still high-end scale, larger medical practices, such as Boca Raton Florida's MDVIP, which opened in 2001, feature a host of doctors who are available exclusively to patients who pay an annual fee of $1,500 or so (on top of regular medical fees) for such healthy perks as guaranteed same-day appointments and home delivery of medications.

THE VOICE OF THE CUSTOMER
BE AT MY SERVICE.

I admit it, sometimes I can be a pest. But hey, I've got a right to great service. Without my business, you'd be out of business. I'm willing to pay for it if I have to, but I expect you to meet me more than halfway. Give me the basics up-front, don't make me beg for them. And let me get more help if I need it, without throwing me out on the street just for asking.

Here are a few suggestions. . . .

- **Be up-front with your help.** I don't want to have to call a long-distance number just to ask a simple question, and I don't want to have to hire a translator to understand how to put together my son's new bike. This isn't rocket science, so don't make me work to get just a little help here.

- **Deliver for me.** Know what I love most about my local pizza place (other than the crusts?). They deliver right to my door. Ditto with my morning paper, and my mail. And now I can even rent DVDs online at Netflix and have them delivered right to my house, cheap and fast (and no late fees if I take a while to return them). Now that's service! So if you've got something I want that you can deliver, send it my way.

- **Okay, I'll pay extra!** I don't expect a free ride. Or full-scale training at rock-bottom prices. If it costs you more, then it seems reasonable that it should cost me more. That's fair. Just tell me up-front what this extra level of service will cost me, so I don't have any surprises when the bill arrives.

- **Let me take it slow.** On a good day, I may want to drink in the scenery, do a bit of window-shopping, or stop and smell the flowers. But are you ready for the relaxed me? Do you have a place where I can wait while my spouse tries on a new outfit? Or where I can cuddle up and read a book, sip a cup of coffee, or hang out with my pals? That's the brilliance of the cafés in bookstores like Border's and Barnes and Noble: They make me feel at home, and they give me a chance to unwind.

Consumers are savvy enough to know whether they're getting their money's worth, so companies should avoid hanging a hefty price-tag on 24/7 access and support, unless they are providing an evidently greater sense of value in return for the premium pricing. Customers who pay more for extended support should clearly be getting a wider and deeper range of services, including more exclusive access to expert assistance, in-home support, and other help that goes above and beyond the normal call of duty.

On the flip side, companies or organizations that pass along their support costs through coercion—by offering no real help or access unless the customer pays for it—are asking for trouble. A common frustration in recent years, especially among technophobes and computer newbies, is the experience of lengthy on-hold, long-distance waits for tech support from a software or computer company. Anyone who's ever paid a stratospheric long-distance bill after getting trapped on phone tech-support hold with a company a thousand miles away will think twice before buying from that company again.

THE VOICE OF THE CUSTOMER
IS ANYBODY THERE?

So, you think that now that you've installed your super-duper phone system, you can automate messages to callers about everything from how to open a new account to how to order an annual report, right? Not so fast! When was the last time you called your company undercover? If you got to where you needed to get in less than 30 seconds, then you did better than I do on most days. Sometimes the "best" phone systems you can buy are the worst for me.

Here's how to untangle my phone cord. . . .

■ **Get a good menu.** I'm not a huge fan of having to press a bunch of numbers only to get more and more recordings that make less and less sense. You can make my life easier by making your menu of options as simple and direct as possible. You probably get enough calls to figure out what people like me are calling about, so make it easier for me to dial up what I need.

■ **Where, oh where, did my "0" option go?** I loved the "0." Sometimes I just want to skip the recordings and cut to the chase by talking with a real live human being. But you don't let me do that anymore, and I'm feeling miffed. Give me back the fallback option, at least as a last resort if I work my way through your system and wind up at a dead end.

■ **How long is this wait, anyway?** First you put me on hold, then you forget I'm here. You subject me to bad elevator music while I wait and wait and wait, without a clue of when you'll be back. And sometimes I'm paying long-distance charges for this alleged "service." If I'm going to have to wait, at least have the courtesy to tell me how long, and how many callers there are ahead of me. Or give me the option of leaving my number, so you can call me back (on your dime). Or tell me when to call back for faster service. Whatever you do, don't just leave me hanging there on perpetual hold! Clue me in, and I'll be grateful for the courtesy.

Fortunately, both for companies and for their customers, the killer combo of new technologies and old-fashioned courtesies can help to bridge the gaping gaps of time, place, and access.

On the technology side, CRM systems allow for intuitive automated responses, virtual agent assistance, and the staging and routing of emails or calls to live support staff. Well-deployed systems also can help build organic knowledge bases, to collect and organize commonly asked questions and responses and thereby assist in the creation of self-help content, such as FAQs, for posting on Web sites, which can reduce call-center traffic by proactively addressing frequent customer questions and problems.

One of the most effective ways of streamlining communications is by integrating existing systems and combining forces so that resources are more effectively deployed toward the mission of customer care. That means doing a better job of mining data and of making sure that customer-service personnel have access to the most complete possible picture of a customer, so they can understand and serve his needs.

Technology is only as good as the people who are using it to connect with consumers, however. You can provide solid customer service just by having a pleasant and well-trained rep-

TECHNOLOGY IS ONLY AS GOOD AS THE PEOPLE WHO ARE USING IT TO CONNECT WITH CONSUMERS.

resentative sitting in front of the phone to answer customer calls. But you can't really offer a quality customer-service experience if all you have on the other end of the line is a database sitting on a server in an empty building. The person at the keyboard or switchboard is the all-important human element; remove him or her, and you remove the human touch that makes all the difference for consumers who need to know there's really something there, when they're dealing with a brand they can't experience in person.

As with everything else companies do to improve their consumer experiences, the importance of great customer service is both a message that needs to be transmitted and a behavior that has to be modeled and mandated from the top of an organization on down. A watchful manager or tuned-in executive who cares deeply about the dynamics of customer support sets the tone and inspires the passion of the whole workforce.

This is essentially what has happened at Pet Warehouse, a catalog and e-commerce pet-supply company based in Dayton, Ohio. The company, which was sold in 2001 to Drs. Foster & Smith, has gained a sterling reputation for fast, friendly, and informed customer support. It's a legacy that can be traced straight to the top of the company: Founder and president Don Laden was known around the office for keeping a close watch over the customer-service lines. If it looked like too many customers were waiting for help, he would pick up the phone himself (even during company meetings) and take customer calls. And everyone else in the company was trained to do same thing. That's the kind of deeply ingrained corporate philosophy that goes a long way toward making 24/7 customer care an innate part of companywide culture.

Companies that care enough to supply their consumers with ever-present support, service, and access do more than simply build goodwill and strengthen relationships. They prove that they're in the trenches with their customers for the long haul, always at the ready, no matter the time or place.

Getting the **24/7** Demandment right at every level, every touch point, every time, is mission-critical in a world where consumers are expecting more, not less, from the brands they associate with—every day, night, and weekend.

There's no time like now, and no place like the top, to start making consumers an around-the-clock priority. So what are you waiting for? The clock is ticking!

DEMANDMENT 06: 24/7—SELF-EVALUATION

Now that you've read this Demandment, see how you stack up. The checkpoints in this form reflect the key takeaways from the "Voice of the Customer" sections. Identify where your company could stand some improvement, and you'll have a shot at building bridges with the people who keep you in business.

6. PUT ME IN CHARGE	Excellent	Good	Poor
Remove the walls.	Consumers can access information about company and get support, 24/7.	Consumers can access information about company 24/7, and leave a message.	Consumers have access to company only during traditional business hours.
I need it *now!*	Consumers have access options for making last-minute purchases, and out-of-stock items can be ordered and shipped overnight.	Consumers have access options for making last-minute purchases.	Consumers have ready access only to a physical store inventory.
Be at my service.	Deliver products and services to the consumers' doorsteps, or by other instantaneous-delivery means.	Deliver products and services to the consumers' doorsteps.	Products are not available by delivery or on demand.
Is anybody there?	Provide stream-lined phone menu, with wait information and ready access to a live rep.	Provide streamlined phone menu and ready access to a live rep.	Consumers have access only to a cumbersome phone menu, and no link to live rep.

The Seventh Demandment

get to know me

TO BORROW A PHRASE made famous by the novelist Anne Tyler, we've become a society of accidental tourists, cocooned in a prefab land where burgers taste the same from chain to chain, all the malls have identical stores, and all the multiplexes are showing the same movies, no matter how far you drive down the highway or how close you stay to home.

In our suburbanized world of franchised restaurants, doc-in-a-box HMOs, and supersized stores, there's a certain convenience and even comfort in this bland consistency. But this one-size-fits-all culture also is alienating, often making us feel anonymous and uniform. Lost in a crowd of look-alike experiences, we feel like look-alike customers, treated like data sets instead of unique individuals.

On the road to our shared standard of living, we've lost the endearing duality of individuality and belonging that once was a natural part of life in a small town or bustling neighborhood. And in light of the growing dangers of our times, not knowing those around us or becoming disconnected from our communities goes beyond the loss of homespun neighborliness to take on more sinister implications.

At the same time we're being asked to provide more and more information about ourselves: our interests, our preferences, our demographics, our backgrounds. And yet even with all of this information-gathering going on, we're not really seeing a huge change in how we're treated. It's as if there's a giant disconnect between what companies think they know about us as sets of consumers, and what they really know about us as people.

So climb up out of the data-mines and into the sunlight of sincerity to interact with your consumers the old-fashioned way: by listening to them, learning from them, and understanding them, not as demographics but as individuals. The Seventh Demandment is **Get to Know Me.** And this time, it's personal.

Recent techno-trends aside, getting to know your consumers isn't about collecting their data or crunching their numbers or clustering their neighborhoods. It's about looking into their eyes and seeing into their lives so as to understand what matters to them, what moves them, and what concerns them.

The Second Demandment—**Inspire Me**—spotlights the emotional ties that can connect and intertwine companies and their consumers;

the Seventh Demandment, **Get to Know Me,** is about bridging the anonymity gap, giving people a sense of individuality and importance by tailoring experiences, products, and services to their unique needs and wants. This Demandment is about clearing away the clutter of the crowd and listening closely when consumers tell companies, "Stop selling to 'them' and start paying attention to *me.*"

Consumers still want to be treated consistently and fairly, no matter who they are or where they shop; but they also expect that, based on their unique needs, companies will get to know them well enough to give them an experience that matters to them, without the vanilla flavoring (unless that's their favorite flavor). And for those who prefer chocolate? "We know our consumers, and understand what occasion [is driving] their purchase," says Milton Matthews, Vice President and Chief Customer Office for the Hershey Foods Corporation. "Are they purchasing out of hunger? Is it nostalgia? Is it romance? We study the consumer because we want to be sure that we can answer each one of their needs on every one of their occasions."

※ THE VOICE OF THE CUSTOMER
THE WORLD REVOLVES AROUND ME.

Me. Not you. Not "them." *Me.* It sounds selfish and I suppose it is but that's the way I see it. That means I want you to listen to *me* when I call, look *me* in the eye when I have a question, help *me* find what I'm looking for. Make *me* feel as if you've dropped everything to tend to *me* individually, and not en masse, and I'll take notice. When your world revolves around *me,* we both gain momentum.

Many companies recognize that they need to do a better job of defining their extremely varied consumers and of treating them as such; and some have gone top-heavy with technology, to crunch out profiles by the pound in an attempt to solve this conundrum. But the very technologies and data-collection capabilities that give us so much information (yet, often, so little understanding) about consumers are also stifling the simple human interactions that can make all the difference in "you-to-me" marketing.

"You-to-me" marketing repersonalizes the idea first developed by Don Peppers and Martha Rogers with their "one-to-one" marketing approach, which helped revolutionize the field. Because numbers are increasingly becoming part of the problem instead of part of the solution, it's easier to grow consumer relationships if you think in terms of "you" and "me" instead of "one" and "one." After all, are you a "one?" Do you even know any "ones?" Not likely.

To see your consumers as people, you've got to set aside the digits and data and get acquainted with their real lives, and their real names. "You-to-me" marketing forces companies to think like their consumers. When consumers think of *you* (that is, your company), they're connecting up with your unique brand experience, not just one more numbered outline on a mall-store map. And to build a relationship with *me,* you've got to see me as more than merely "one" among many other ones.

It may seem a subtle distinction. But step outside the box, take a breath of fresh air, and you'll realize that even such simple changes as moving language from "one-to-one" to "you-to-me" can shift thinking and set the stage for greater intimacy with your consumers.

One of the best ways to understand what consumers want and need from your brand is to watch them interact with your own brand experience in your mutual natural habitat: your store, your Web site, or wherever they make contact with your brand. How do they react to what you're offering? How do your associates react to them?

What displays, pages, or categories are consumers gravitating toward or steering away from? What kinds of questions are they asking? What kinds of answers are they getting? How many are browsing versus buying, and do your associates treat the browsers differently? Where else do they shop, and what's that experience like? And when was the last time you interacted anonymously with your brand, to see precisely what consumers see when they experience it? Take a look at your consumers' behavior within the context of your brand, to see what's really going on when they experience your world.

THE VOICE OF THE CUSTOMER
LIVE IN MY SHOES.

Put 'em on. Walk around. How do they feel? Too tight, too loose, or maybe a tad clunky? Okay, maybe you don't need to actually *wear* my shoes, but truly understanding the world as it is seen from my perspective may actually change your own. My life—the things I care about, the company I keep, the work I do, the way I play—tells a story about me that no amount of factoids could create.

So tie those laces and take a stroll in my shoes. . . .

■ **Don't ask who I am, watch what I do.** Survey after survey asks me what I think, what I want, what I buy, what I need. That's okay, but really I'd rather you saw me as a person instead of as a form I've filled out. It's like secretly hoping your partner will choose the perfect holiday gift without even having to ask you for a wish list. Look at me, not just at my information, and you'll get to know me faster.

■ **Get out of the lab and into my life.** Drive my car, sit at my desk, run my errands. Or just take notice of my morning routine as I search for matching socks, wrestle my kids out of a deep sleep, frantically pack lunches that vaguely comprise the major food groups, and eat breakfast standing up even though my own mother taught me otherwise. If you could make a little part of my day just a little bit better by figuring out how to make it easier for me, personally, we'd both win.

Paco Underhill, the founder of Envirosell and the father of the science of retail anthropology, has documented shopper behavior for more than two decades, and gleaned keen insights that have affected retail design and marketing.

In his book, *Why We Buy: The Science of Shopping* (1999), Underhill tells tales from the field about how he and his researchers have uncovered such phenomena as the "butt brush" effect. We have this particular insight to thank for wider aisles, more spacious stores, and less crowded display racks, as Underhill's team documented the evident discomfort of shoppers whose personal (rear) space was invaded while squeezing between narrow aisles of overstocked racks or shelving.

Likewise, the fairly new science of usability is all about observing how people actually interact with Web sites, kiosks, computer-based training, or other media, or systems that require a skilled information design if they are to deliver an easily absorbed and navigated experience. Following a set of established guidelines known as heuristics, usability analysts watch, listen, and learn how typical users explore an experience, then document the trouble-spots that will need improvements.

Consultants and analysts may be doing the watching, but it's the companies doing the hiring that show their consumer-oriented savvy. Procter & Gamble may be head and shoulders above the crowd in many ways, but their innovative consumer research and marketing initiatives have helped it get close to its consumers in real and virtual settings alike. The company's Consumer & Market Knowledge division studies consumer needs through real-world observation, while its Web site is used to gather consumer feedback on new and existing products.

Sometimes getting to know consumers means holding up a mirror to them, so they can see themselves through your eyes. Giving them the power

SOMETIMES KNOWING WHO YOUR CUSTOMERS *AREN'T* IS JUST AS IMPORTANT AS KNOWING WHO THEY ARE.

to access, update, and change their information not only saves you money on data-cleansing, it also provides you with additional opportunities to ask about personal preferences and to capture further consumer information.

THE VOICE OF THE CUSTOMER
TELL ME HOW MUCH BUSINESS I DID WITH YOU.

I admit it, sometimes I don't keep as close a watch on where my money goes as I should. But I expect that the folks I fork it over to will know where it's going. So I'd really like to know how much I spend with you over time. Sure, I could tally my checkbook or run a report on Quicken. But there's something special about getting a year-end summary of our relationship, like I do from American Express.

I might be a bit stunned at how much I spent, and on what I spent it, but still I'll really appreciate the fact that you cared enough to keep track for me and with me. When you take the time to summarize my spending and to send the summary to me (or give me online access to that info), I feel that you see our relationship in terms of a partnership, not just as a series of one-sided transactions.

Paradoxically (or is it, myopically?), to see consumers up close, companies have to take a step back and view them in the context of the ongoing stories of their lives.

That's why the *"Get to"* part of **Get to Know Me** is an important aspect of this Demandment. It evokes the journey companies must take alongside their consumers. The Tenth Demandment—**Stay with Me**—explores this idea in greater depth, but in essence, long-term consumer relationships depend on the companies' agility in providing products and services that meet the evolving needs of their consumers over time.

People's lives move along a continuum: As their lives change, their interests change; as their circumstances change, their needs change. Most women read bridal magazines only when they're planning a wedding, for instance. They have a deep, if brief, interest in the subject matter, and then they move on to the new set of interests, needs, and challenges that comes along with married life.

So while you may think you know your consumers collectively, or even as individuals, if you're not frequently revising your understanding of who they are becoming based on where they are going and where they have been, your company is all too likely to lose sight of their shifting priorities and needs.

Of course, it never hurts to start with a rough sketch of a consumer's life and lifestyle, so as to prepare the canvas for the more detailed attitudinal and behavioral portrait to come. That's why the right kinds of data and demographics can help you to draw an outline that gets filled in over time with more personal interactions and insights. Where a person lives—in a retirement home, a singles' community, or an active family neighborhood—as well as what their racial or ethnic background is, where they grew up, where they went to school (and how much school they attended), what they do for a living, how many children they have—all of these factors are elements that add up to an initial outline of a consumer's needs and interests.

Sometimes, knowing who your consumers *aren't* is just as important as knowing who they are. And success comes from knowing how and where to draw the line between those two camps. That's how The Limited, Inc. has been able to be so successful with strong fashion brands such as Express, as well as Victoria's Secret.

"I want some brand rejecters," explains Dan Finkelman, The Limited, Inc.'s Senior Vice President for Brand and Business Planning. "I want some people to say about Express or Victoria's Secret, 'That's not for me.' Because if you're for everyone, then you're not fashion. You're not sticking out as a unique place in today's marketplace. You're a commodity. The moment you commoditize, the whole magic of the brand experience starts to decompose."

In any relationship, getting to know somebody means understanding where the boundaries are and how to avoid crossing over them. What that means for consumers is that there's a big difference between a personalized experience and a too-personal encounter. The attempt to walk that fine line can befuddle even the most sophisticated of companies, especially those trying to build sensitive and timely profiles of their customers so that they can better serve their needs (and get some info on buying behavior for wider company use). As mentioned in the First Demandment, **Earn My Trust,** the

✳ VICTORIA'S SECRET—SECRETS OF THE SEXIEST BRAND ON EARTH

What other brand could make angels sexy, bring the bedroom out of the closet and into malls and mailboxes, and shut down the Web with a Webcast that attracted millions of visitors? And all with just a little fabric and a lot of Victoria Secret's attitude?

A brand with almost superhuman strength and a potent, confident sensuality, it knows no boundaries, either in channels or media. A global power with store, catalogue, and Web customer touch points, it was the first major apparel brand in history to strut its stuff in a primetime network TV fashion show—and a hugely successful one at that.

Victoria's Secret, or VS as it is known to industry insiders, has managed to extend its brand and audience into almost every nook and cranny of the shopping and fashion entertainment world.

So, what *is* VS's key to success (other than the obvious—the world's most beautiful women wearing lingerie)? In large part, it's the strong brand management that defines and protects the brand experience while carefully tending its growth. "The brand really is the sum and substance of all the influences that touch a customer," says Dan Finkelman, Senior Vice President for Brand and Business Planning for The Limited, Inc.

"Whether it's direct contact with your brand, the advertising or imagery, the use of the product or the store experience . . . all of that formulates the emotive connection with the customer. Anything that influences that is part of the brand experience."

"Clearly," he adds, "the process by which you articulate what you want for the brand—the direction and the brand definition—creates clear boundaries, guidelines, and directions in which to go," says Finkelman.

And a strong understanding of the customer is equally important to the success of the brand. "If you don't understand customers, you're dead. And that's the secret to the retail side of the equation."

Inherent in understanding the customer is an awareness of how her needs and tastes are changing throughout her life. "Because lifestyle changes, your body-type changes, your fashion sense changes, and . . . the pocket book changes. There isn't anything that can happen to you, necessarily, that doesn't change your relationship to one of our brands," Finkelman says.

Which is why the company spends so much time understanding the lives and everyday needs of its customers. "How do they live? What's their life like? How did they react to the store, catalogue, or Web site? How do they wear and use our merchandise? . . . This is what we want to know more about."

But one thing they know for sure is that the Victoria's Secret customer has hopes and dreams that the company seems to be able to fulfill. The image the brand projects to customers, Finkelman says, is "always, always, always aspirational. Period."

bottom line is this: Don't ask questions or demand information that's either out of place or too personal in nature.

Part of the problem is that personalization technology—designed to shape the delivery of experiences uniquely suited to an individual's preferences or interests—is still in its infancy, and thus immaturely overdependent on hard data collected directly from consumers, as opposed to information developed through inference and behavioral observation. Once the technology evolves to a more intuitive, organic level where we can better learn about individuals from the way they shop or browse, the need for this kind of semiintrusive data collection should decrease.

But in the meantime, companies attempting to use personalization technologies to improve their consumer experiences may be doing their brands, and their consumers, a disservice if they resort to hamhanded attempts at cataloging their consumers' stats. When a magazine asks about a new subscriber's household income, or a cosmetics salesperson requests a consumer's phone number when she's just buying a tube of lipstick, the alarm bells will ring as many consumers ask, "Why do you need to know *that*?"

Even if you're making perfectly reasonable requests for information, always give your consumers something back for their donation of personal data. That's where the "New ROI," or Return on Information, comes into play. This new meaning for an old acronym transforms the idea of ROI into a consumer-centric measurement that forces companies to ask themselves what they are really doing to benefit consumers in exchange for all the data they collect about them.

Companies that put a strong emphasis on delivering a new ROI to their consumers are showing that they value their input and that they really are using the information gathered to build more personal or meaningful experiences for their consumers. And consumers are willing to share more information about themselves, despite concerns about privacy and abuse of their data, if they believe they'll be getting something in return.

THERE'S A BIG DIFFERENCE BETWEEN A PERSONAL EXPERIENCE AND A TOO-PERSONAL ENCOUNTER.

THE VOICE OF THE CUSTOMER
TAKE IT SLOW.

You know my name, and that can be both comforting and concerning. It's comforting to be recognized or remembered. I mean, who *doesn't* like to hear or see their name? I'm taken aback, and pleasantly surprised, when Nine West and others send promotional emails with my name in the subject line, not just the greeting. Maybe I get the same offer as every other customer, but I still feel special. Yet sometimes these tricks can ring hollow, especially when my name is botched, when I'm barraged with sensitive personal questions, or when companies make suggestions that have nothing to do with my preferences.

According to a Personalization Consortium study, 51 percent of the consumers asked said they would share their personal information in return for better service. When asked what they would share in exchange for a more customized experience, 76 percent of consumers surveyed said they would provide information about their tastes, interests, and hobbies; 81 percent would share their addresses; 95 percent would give out their email addresses; and 96 percent would provide their names.

That same study showed that consumers didn't like being asked the same questions over and over again. Sixty-two percent of respondents said they dislike Web sites that ask for personal information they have already provided, and 73 percent said they would find it useful for sites to remember their information. And it's not just a Web problem. A company with multiple channels won't make its consumers very happy if they have to provide the same information again and again—in stores, on the phone, and online. One database, one view—period. That's what consumers now demand.

Developing and maintaining a single view of your customers not only cuts down on their frustration, it also reduces the likelihood of conflicting data-sets that need constant cleansing and purging. Still, it can cost a small fortune to make this happen, so some companies may need to wait until the implementation costs have come down to a point where the business benefits outweigh the investment costs. But once enabled, this single view of a consumer's data not only gives companies a better perspective on overall buying habits, it also lets them meet and greet their consumers not as strangers but as old friends, no matter where or when they show up.

THE VOICE OF THE CUSTOMER
SEE ME AS ONE CUSTOMER.

I don't know how you're organized. Are you one company with three ways to buy? Or one company with separate, competing divisions? Three companies? Quite honestly, I don't care. I simply see you as one brand. One brand offering me many ways to interact, to buy, and to get service. As a result, I want you to see me as one customer. One customer with one relationship with you—not several disparate relationships.

Here's how to prove you can count backward to one. . . .

■ **Don't make me tell you twice.** I know, I know: Forms make the world go 'round. I've resigned myself to a life of filling out little boxes with my name and personal info. But if you've asked me for that info before, don't ask me to repeat it again and again, unless it's for accuracy or updating. Physicians love to give me repetitive paperwork, as does my bank; so do the public schools. I long for the day where I can hand my info over at the touch of a single button—but one that only I can push.

■ **Keep a record—one record.** Apparently this one must be tough for you, because no one seems to do it yet. I patronize your stores, your catalog, and your Web site, but you don't seem to realize it. I buy products from a broad range of categories, but you send me news and coupons only for one. Or worse, if I do business with you in several areas, I often get separate, inconsistent communications. Consolidate your view of me so that you don't waste my time—or make me wonder if my loyalty is being wasted on a company that hasn't even noticed it yet.

■ **Remember me when I come back.** Find a way to recognize me when I return. Know what I like, or have ready access to my purchase history. I may be one of your best customers, but your sales associates probably don't know it. Let me scan my customer card so you can retrieve my info, make suggestions, and provide more specialized attention to me on a given day.

Personal contact, and personalized experience, are two very different things. Addressing a consumer by her name is *not* the same as addressing her needs. Logging onto a site that welcomes someone back by using her first name isn't a quality experience in and of itself, unless the site is also offering genuinely relevant information that shows the company knows more about the consumer than her name or the last thing she bought there.

Likewise, telemarketers can leave a bad taste in consumers' mouths when they use someone's first name during a call, or otherwise act familiar or chummy. Even in this informal day and age that privilege normally comes only through some sort of personal acquaintance, and consumers know who they know and who they don't.

The personal touch often is welcome, though, when a customer walks into a store, hotel lobby, restaurant, repair shop, or doctor's office, and is greeted by name. It makes customers feel that somehow they've been remembered. That they're in their own personal version of *Cheers,* where everybody knows their name.

Harrah's, the hotel and casino company, is perfecting the art of this kind of customer greeting and knowledge-base. The company has instituted a heavy-duty customer-relationship program at its properties, with an eye toward meeting guests' needs by knowing them as well as possible. So when a returning guest walks into a Harrah's hotel, he can be warmly greeted before he even announces himself (thanks to a discrete stash of photos at the reception desk, showing the regular customers who are expected to check in that day). Once he gets to his rooms, he'll find the bar stocked with his favorite beverages, extra pillows if he's asked for them before, and other personal touches that show how well Harrah's knows what he wants and needs while staying with them.

Of course, having a store clerk garble your name when handing you back your credit card is a bit of a bubble-buster, so every attempt at this kind of personalized greeting or attention needs to come across as genuine; otherwise, it may well ring false as a merely mandated pleasantry.

As with the other consumer Demandments, technology—and the Internet in particular—has altered the landscape of consumer relationships by giving people experiences, services, and product options tailored to their tastes and needs as never before. And as with many of the other Demandments, this personal turn of events is not so much a revolution in consumer empowerment as it is a renaissance of those old-fashioned values and relationships that were once a part of our everyday life.

The Internet has brought our modern world full-circle by providing more direct ways for companies and consumers to interact, even while automating that process through technologies that collect, organize, and manage the data and communications that allow for more targeted profiling and customized experiences. And with the advent of back-end manufacturing systems that make possible smaller-batch production and the custom-packaging of everything from print-on-demand (POD) books to made-to-fit Lands' End chinos, many businesses are now able to create customer-customized products en masse.

Amazon.com fired one of the first shots in the personalization revolution simply by putting its Web site on a first-name basis with visitors—welcoming returning customers with a greeting that showed that the site "recognized" them. And Amazon.com has maintained the online lead in delivering experiences that have become increasingly tailored to individual customers' interests and buying habits, even down to serving up dynamically generated ministore pages that reflect the recent products and site areas a consumer has visited.

Pure players may have set the standard, but long-established companies have turned to the Web to find ways to target-market to customers in a way that never have been possible without the online tools of profiling databases and related technologies. Procter & Gamble's Reflect.com sells custom-blended cosmetics and skin-care products that even come packaged with color schemes chosen by the customers. And with every selection, every choice, and every purchase, customers are showing and telling Reflect.com more and more about themselves—interactions that eventually are reflected in more meaningful experiences for customers.

"There are two primary ways that we get to know our customer," explains Hannelore Schmidt, Reflect.com's Director of Customer Delight and Loyalty. "First, we get to know her through her interaction with our Web site. As she creates products, she can answer over 100 different questions about her beauty needs and desires." But that's only part of the process for understanding customers, Schmidt says.

"The second way we get to know her is through her interaction with our Concierge Service. Although we can't flow that information back into the Web site, our Concierge team can see all the interactions that the customer has had with us, and uses that information to give her the best experience possible."

But beauty isn't the only thing getting more personal online. So is breakfast. General Mills' mycereal.com lets cereal-lovers create their own personal breakfast treat with ingredients they select on the site and then save for future orders. And shoes are in the online news, too. At Nike.com's Nike iD store, athletes can make their mark on a personalized pair of shoes by configuring their own style and color schemes and then imprinting their name.

These companies aren't really creating personalized merchandise for individual consumers; they are simply producing products based on a consumer's preferred configuration. Still, the end-products are a heck of a lot closer to "made for me" than off-the-shelf stock.

Companies that lack such customization capabilities are using demographics and data in other ways to fulfill the increasingly fragmented needs that come with America's growing diversity of lifestyles. The explosion of niche marketing for niche products in the past decade shows how companies are striving to adapt themselves to newly perceived or emerging market segments just large enough to support a brand or product line of their own. So from instant oatmeal, fortified to meet women's nutritional needs, to NASCAR-shaped universal remote-control devices, stores are overflowing with specialty products aimed at almost every demographic under the sun.

What determines the arrangement or the assortment on those shelves is just as important as the assortment itself. Grocery stores near college campuses are likely to stock more alternative foods, while those in ethnic neighborhoods will have foods and products targeted toward the local population.

Even the store architecture itself may change, depending on the neighborhood or the environment. The Lakeland, Florida-based Publix Stores are setting about blending in better (if dramatically) with their settings as they build or redesign new stores. The company worked for over a year with the Riverside Avondale Preservation Society (which upholds the architectural integrity of a historic neighborhood in Jacksonville, Florida) to come up with a store design that blended in with the community's look and feel. Far less subdued, but also appropriate to its neighborhood, is the Publix

❋ CUTTING THE MUSTARD: CONDIMENTAL CONSUMERISM

When you market a niche product line, you probably already know your niche market. And it's hard to get any niche-ier than mustard. Just ask Barry Levenson, proprietor of the Mount Horeb (Wisc.) Mustard Museum, which displays more than 3700 mustards and mustard-related artifacts and sells thousands of mustard-related SKUs in an adjacent store, as well as through a witty catalog and Web site that take the idea of food fetishes to a whole new level.

Levenson, a lawyer who served as Wisconsin's Assistant Attorney General (and once argued a case before the U.S. Supreme Court with a jar of lucky mustard in his pocket—and won!) left the law in 1991 to devote his energies to his true passion. He opened his mustard museum and store the following year.

But he's not alone in his spicy obsession. His love of mustard has spread to thousands of loyal clientele, including more than 50 customers who subscribe to his "Mustard of the Month Club," which each month delivers a hand-selected shipment of specialty mustards to its members.

So who *are* these consummate condiment consumers? "They tend to be a little quirky," says Levenson. "And they're people with very special tastes. They like things to be just exactly right for them. And they tend to have higher income levels—after all, we're talking about specialty mustards, not grocery mustards. People are spending six or seven dollars apiece on these, instead of a dollar or two in the grocery store. But it's an affordable luxury: Something that people won't deny themselves, because they really enjoy how special it is."

Levenson also has noticed that his customers often are health-conscious: "A lot of people now are into mustard because it has virtually no calories and no fat." But they're not keeping it all to themselves, either.

"They're also very giving people. They love to share. And word of mouth in the specialty mustard industry is really a key to its success."

Levenson's hottest line, so to speak, in his gift collection of "personalized" mustards—which feature labels bearing the name and photograph of the recipient or giver. "We're just having a lot of fun with that, and so are our customers," he says.

Levenson believes that part of the appeal of the unusual mustards he sells—which range in flavor from Wasabi lime, to red jalapeno and lavender honey, to mango butter— is their small-batch quality and the dedication to craftsmanship. "These small mustard companies are so passionate about what they do," he says. "To me, a lot of the small companies are like the old aviator buffs from a hundred years ago. They're totally into what they're doing. It's all-consuming for them. And my customers relate to that passion for perfection."

Oh, and there's one more thing Levenson thinks sets his customers apart from the lesser herd of ketchup or mayo devotees: "They have a sense of humor. There's just something about mustard that makes people smile."

store in Miami's trendy South Beach Art Deco district: the traffic-stopping building looks like the *Titanic!*

Niches go beyond neighborhoods, of course. And car companies, which have long marketed station wagons or sports cars to particular types of buyers, now are steering a new course in niche marketing by focusing on consumers who have yet to be fully tapped for their loyalty potential. Subaru, for instance, has gained a reputation as a gay-and-lesbian-friendly car maker by, among other things, serving as a founding sponsor for the Rainbow Endowment (chaired by Martina Navratilova, it raises money for gay and lesbian causes) through an affinity credit-card program called "the Rainbow Card." Likewise, companies can effectively engage the awareness of niche markets through event sponsorship or fundraising efforts that reflect the tastes and interests of their consumers.

The Second Demandment—**Inspire Me**—takes on issues of cause-related marketing, but event sponsorship and fundraising efforts are relevant in this Demandment as well, because they're all about connecting with your customers by knowing who they are, what they're about, and where they're hanging out. That's why, although you won't see Mountain Dew® sponsoring performances of the New York City Ballet, you can't miss their logo plastered all over events associated with the extreme sport-oriented "X Games."

Tide laundry detergent has been actively involved in youth soccer programs for years. But it's not the sport itself that matters; it's what happens during the game that counts to the brand. "That's where kids get dirty," says Tide's Brand Manager Brian McNamara; "but it's also a big thing in the United States, and something that's important to parents and to kids." And therefore, it's important to Tide. "I constantly get calls from professional soccer teams because they've heard that Tide's interested in soccer," he adds. "But that's not Tide. We're not in soccer because we want to be connected to soccer. We're in soccer because we want to be connected to our consumers."

Knowing your consumers also means not showing off if you know more than they do. Consumers out shopping for their first computer, kicking the tires on a possible new car,

KNOWING YOUR CONSUMERS ALSO MEANS NOT SHOWING OFF IF YOU KNOW MORE THAN THEY DO.

or even just stopping in for a cup of coffee shouldn't have to carry a glossary or dictionary around to understand what your associates are saying to them. Yes, they want your expert opinion, but no, they don't want it in a language they can't understand. After all, as noted by Ann Hanson, Vice President of Marketing and Sales for Ford Motor Co.'s TH!NK Mobility division—which in 2001 rolled out a multilanguage Web site for European consumers: "You can only talk to people in a language they understand."

THE VOICE OF THE CUSTOMER
SPEAK MY LANGUAGE.

You may not realize it, but you're speaking a foreign language to me with your scientific ingredients, your technobabble, and your insider's acronyms. When you rattle on like that, I don't even know how to ask about what I'm looking for or need help with. So start making sense by lightening up on the intimidating double-talk, so I'm able to understand you.

Here's how to talk my way. . . .

■ **Limit your lingo.** Physicians are the worst—always using Latin terms for even the mildest of maladies. But lawyers and techies can be just as bad as Trekkies when it comes to speaking in tongues not my own. Even coffeehouses leave me steamed these days. Other than Frasier Crane, who's really sure what a grande, decaf mocha, with soy and no cream, tastes like? And watch out if you dare to speak Starbucks lingo in a Caribou coffee house . . . they're likely to call in a moose hunter to take you down! I understand that you're an authority and trying to create a special effect that enhances that aura, but talk to me in a way that makes sense to me; you can return to your own planet later on.

■ **Translation, please.** I'm not overly impressed by overly complex instructions, counterintuitive product design, buzzwordy labeling, or obtuse signs and symbols. But you're such a pro, you often don't realize when I'm not with you. So if you must make things hard to understand, at least spare me the embarrassment of asking you to translate. Offer pronunciations, provide me with a glossary, show me pictures, or give me vivid descriptions so I can make my way through your world with at least a bit of dignity.

Customers don't care about having a personalized experience so much as they care about having a *meaningful* one. Which is to say, meaningful on a personal level. That's why, for all the bells and whistles of the Internet and CRM, what really counts in the long run is the sense of being known as an individual, understood as a unique human being, and treated with the respect that each and every one of us deserves.

So . . . whatcha gonna do if you're stuck down on the data farm when all of your customers are window-shopping out on Main Street, longing for some old-fashioned face-to-face time with real people who know and care about them?

The rule here is that you can't get to know people in

YOU CAN ONLY TALK TO PEOPLE IN A LANGUAGE THEY UNDERSTAND.

**Ann Hanson,
Ford Motor Co.**

a vacuum, and they can't get to know you. Maybe that's why a 2001 poll showed that 86 percent of people who bought products online were buying established brands that they already knew and trusted.

And if consumers feel that the brands they know and trust also know them back and are giving them the products and services they really want and need as a result . . . well, companies in the know realize that that's the ultimate bond.

DEMANDMENT 07: **GET TO KNOW ME—SELF-EVALUATION**

Now that you've read this Demandment, see how you stack up. The checkpoints in this form reflect the key takeaways from the "Voice of the Customer" sections. Identify where your company could stand some improvement, and you'll have a shot at building bridges with the people who keep you in business.

7. GET TO KNOW ME	Excellent	Good	Poor
The world revolves around *me*.	Company or company reps routinely treat consumers as unique individuals.	Company or company reps often treat consumers as unique individuals.	Each consumer is treated like the next.
Live in my shoes.	Routinely observe consumers behavior in their world, to understand them better.	Routinely conduct consumer surveys, to understand them better.	Rarely ask consumers' opinions or observe behavior.
Tell me how much business I did with you.	Provide summary of annual spending, and category breakdowns.	Summary of spending to date, sent upon request.	Don't keep track of consumers' cumulative spending.
Take it slow.	Companies use customers' identifying information over time, and with caution, to build a relationship.	Companies use customers' identifying information with caution.	Companies move too quickly, or not at all, to build the relationship.
See me as one customer.	Consolidated view of consumers, regardless of channel, and recognition upon return.	Consolidated view of consumers, regardless of channel.	No integration of consumer records across channels.
Speak my language.	Avoid jargon that intimidates consumers, and translate or illustrate where appropriate.	Avoid jargon that intimidates consumers.	Speak to consumers with jargon, to intentionally intimidate or manipulate.

08

The Eighth Demandment

exceed my expectations

EXPECTATIONS ARE A FUNNY THING: Set them too high, and they're hard to meet. Set them too low, and you're cutting off your proverbial nose to spite your face, by underselling what you have to offer. And in a world where people already expect, well, the world from companies, it's pretty hard to take things up a notch when you feel like you've already ratcheted up your capabilities as high as they can go.

But that's what companies must seek to do if they hope to capture the hearts and minds—and therefore, the loyalty—of today's consumers. You've got to set yourself apart by being even better and trying even harder, if you want to stand out from the crowd of competitors offering the same products and services, or even the same kinds of experiences, as you do.

The Ten Demandments outline ways that companies can stand out by offering outstanding brand experiences—honest, inspirational, accessible, informative, and meaningful—so as to earn consumers' trust and loyalty. Truly memorable products, services, and experiences share a common trait: They go above and beyond what came before, or what they compete against. "Good enough" is *never* enough in a world where consumers demand greatness in everything from a cup of coffee to a cruise vacation.

EXCEEDING EXPECTATIONS IS ABOUT DELIVERING AN EXPERIENCE THAT TRANSCENDS THE ACTUAL PURCHASE OR SERVICE.

That's why the Eighth Demandment, **Exceed My Expectations**, is about launching consumers on their most exciting leap of faith ever, the leap that takes them from trust to loyalty, from expectation to delight. Exceeding expectations is about building an invisible but tenable bridge to the other side of the transactional equation, thereby proving that your company is willing to not only deliver on its original promises but to go the extra mile, to do something out of the ordinary, and far more than necessary to prove, again and again, that your customers will get more than they pay for, or even anticipate, each and every time they do business with you.

And it's about saying you're sorry *before* anyone complains about a minor problem; about being proactive, not reactive, in fixing those little things that aren't quite right; and about making amends in big ways even when a small response would do. In other words it's about being better than you have to be, not only because your consumers expect (or demand) it, but because they *deserve* it.

Perhaps, most importantly, exceeding expectations is about delivering an experience that transcends the actual purchase or service—it's the intangible "*Wow!*" that makes people sit up and take notice, clap their hands in delight, or just want to hug you for getting it not just right, but more than right. Companies that exceed expectations are really exceeding their own limits, reaching higher and trying harder because that's what they do and who they are. Personal bests are challenged and extended when companies exceed their consumers' expectations by overcoming their own limitations.

But, you say, it's hard to exceed expectations, when consumers already have such heightened expectations. And indeed, it is a challenge; after all, much of this book is devoted to helping you deal with the increasingly demanding expectations that today's heavily-marketed-to consumers project onto companies through every channel and in all categories.

That's a tough audience out there—one that's come to expect from most companies, as par for the course, the kinds of special treatment and targeted products, services, technologies, and communications that once would have been unimaginable. Now, companies have to work hard to simply *live up to*—much less *exceed*—their customers' expectations.

Still, that's as it should be. It's a natural part of the experience evolution: Consumer experiences will continue to improve, to enrich, and to deepen, as companies innovate new ways to connect more meaningfully with their customers. Companies that survive and thrive are those that are always working to innovate and to improve the experiences their customers have with their products, services, and touch points. By striving to always exceed expectations, great companies are raising the bar for themselves and others.

Companies that exceed expectations are there for their consumers even when they don't have to be: doing more, trying harder, and showing they care that much more. For instance: They stay open a little longer if a few are still earnestly shopping, rather than brusquely ushering those folks to the door. They send personalized replies to customer letters and emails, as opposed to blanket form responses that reek of automation. They don't charge for a meal if a diner isn't satisfied. They cover shipping costs, wrap a package beautifully, and send a note a few days later to make sure all went well with the delivery. They do more than the right thing—they do the smart thing.

Exceeding expectations isn't about perfection; rather, it's about enthusiastic, relevant responsiveness to consumer needs, even if they haven't been expressed. And even when such a company stumbles, it finds a way to recovering with such grace and generosity that what consumers remember is the thoughtful response, not the mistake that initially triggered it. When McDonald's uncovered a sophisticated scam being run by employees of a company that had been staging its Monopoly™ game giveaway of cash and prizes, the fast-food giant did more than just apologize, or say it wouldn't happen again. Instead it broadcast nationwide apologies and staged a new giveaway of big bucks at its restaurants; clearly, the goal was not just to replace the prize money that hadn't gone to consumers, the first time around, but to regain their trust.

THE VOICE OF THE CUSTOMER
OVERCOMPENSATE.

Okay, so chances are you're not offering the lowest price or the widest selection. And chances are I know this, because I've done my homework by talking to friends, sifting through advertisements, and surfing the Web. So how are you going to entice me now? What ofter ways have you come up with to make up for that one major weakness.

Here's how to counterbalance a shortcoming. . . .

- **Try harder.** A lot harder. It's amazing how I can be drawn in by a company or its associates who go the extra mile. If you're in a bad location and I have to drive a long distance, make it worth my while by killing me with customer-service kindness, by carrying my packages to my car, or by offering me free shipping. My favorite local toy store stands out from the industry giants by offering its signature festive gift-wrapping on all purchases, for free, year-round. If that's not up your alley, show you really care by doing some extra legwork to answer my question, especially if it's beyond your scope of knowledge. Get the picture? When you try harder than you have to, it makes a difference in how I see you.

- **Upgrade your quality.** The devil is in the details. And it's the details I'll notice—and remember. Take travel, for instance. Have you ever tried to actually dry your hair in a hotel using the in-room, wall-mounted appliance? Aaack! The low heat and the short cord make it an agonizing effort. And don't get me started on the narrow desks, dim lighting, weak coffee, thin pillows, and stiff sheets. But then recently I stayed in a run-of-the-mill chain hotel and I was delighted to find that they had an ergonomically designed Aeron chair in the room. I was wowed (and very comfortable while I worked), and now I think better of that hotel than I ever did before. So just know that when you find meaningful ways to upgrade your quality, I'm sure to notice.

BY STRIVING TO ALWAYS EXCEED EXPECTATIONS, GREAT COMPANIES ARE RAISING THE BAR FOR THEMSELVES AND OTHERS. Sometimes, exceeding expectations is as simple as doing something a little (or a lot) better than customers have come to expect from a typical consumer experience—like visiting a car dealership, for instance. Saturn's new showrooms, a far cry from the hard-core sales scene and dreary service-setting most car buyers are accustomed to, offer customers a warm and welcoming living-room environment where they can lounge in leather chairs and sip a latte, or check their email at computer work stations. When they buy a car, the Saturn team celebrates the customer with balloons and applause. And if there's a reason for mass vehicle servicing (such as a recall), the dealers don't just send out notification postcards—they hold barbecues, picnics, or other events that make coming in for mandatory service feel more like a party than a pain in the neck.

That's the kind of exceptional experience that has earned Saturn the highest rating in J. D. Power and Associates' Customer Satisfaction Study every year since 1996. The survey, which measures customer satisfaction with car-buying experiences, has consistently ranked Saturn first, ahead even of luxury carmakers.

It can be a lot easier for nonluxury companies to exceed expectations, of course, because expectations naturally are lower for everyday products, services, and experiences. This expectation-gap offers smart companies tremendous opportunity to jump in and do things differently. It may cost more, but by upgrading a commonplace experience with a few extras and thoughtful touches, companies can leap-frog the competition when the race has just barely begun. That's what Target has managed to do for its shoppers by transforming the discount shopping experience into one that's filled with creative flair and a dash of (dare we say it?) elegance.

For higher-end companies whose reputations have been built on best-in-class experiences, the key to continuing to exceed expectations lies in not only maintaining a legendary level of commitment to customer care, but also in finding new ways to polish that image by keeping the brand fresh and meaningful to consumers in changing times.

Companies renowned for their high levels of customer service—American Express and Neiman-Marcus, come to mind—know that their names alone will take them only so far. The experiences they offer must retain that relevancy, dependability, and glow of greatness for which they have always been known.

When American Express sprang into action to help stranded travelers after the September 11, 2001, terrorist attacks, even though their own corporate offices had been badly damaged in the event, they were living up to and moving beyond the expectations they had set with their card-holders over the years. For many AmEx customers that may well have been the first time they ever needed to avail themselves of the travelers' services the company has so long promoted; but the company's swift, compassionate, and focused response proved that their faith had not been misplaced, and that AmEx was indeed all it said it was, and more.

✳ THE VOICE OF THE CUSTOMER
DO MORE THAN YOU SHOULD.

Sure, you're thinking that trying harder is hard to define, so being as good as you can be is good enough. But don't write this off as something to tackle in the future—when you have more time, more money, or more technology. It should be something you're always thinking about, because when you overdeliver, it sends a message to me loud and clear. A message that you're not just going through the motions with me to make a buck. A message saying that you actually care enough about what you do to give me the kind of experience I really want.

Here's how to keep your eye on the ball. . . .

- **The little things are big.** Everything doesn't have to be a big deal. Sometimes it's the small things that stand out. Simple instruction manuals, IKEA-style. Beautiful pasta-sauce bottles, like those by Barilla, that I can use again later. And do you know what would be stunning? Receiving an email response within minutes detailing a specific answer to my question. Helpful too are appointment-reminder calls and emails, and even that little static sticker on my windshield from Jiffy Lube. And if you want to truly exceed my expectation, send me a bill that's actually lower than your estimate. Now that would be big!

- **I'm more than a billboard.** I know you feel proud, and maybe even a bit smug, when I walk around with your logo in my hand, on my chest, on my head, or in some other highly visible locale. Shamefully I confess I've worn a few t-shirts and sipped coffee out of mugs from companies I've never heard of, let alone cared about. But I don't feel particularly good about it (or about those companies). But when I do care, and when you make it worth my while, I'm happy to become your best messenger. For instance, my favorite neighborhood bookstore sells sweatshirts with their logo on it. And if I'm wearing the sweatshirt when I make a purchase, I get 10 percent off! That's a great give-and-take I don't mind wearing for the world to see.

Times of tragedy tend to bring out the best in people and organizations; but even when things are going smoothly, companies must strive to offer that same level of attention and commitment, whether it means helping a consumer to find a last-minute hotel or to locate a unique gift for a hard-to-please mother-in-law.

In the rarified air of luxury products and services, exceeding expectations by anticipating customer wants and needs is achieved by making good on long-established traditions of customer care, and then evolving as consumers evolve. Going above and beyond, raising the bar without being asked, and continuing to take the lead—those are the hallmarks of all companies that stay ahead of the curve and the competition by knowing just how to make their customers feel cared about, and for, in the short run and over the long haul.

And make no mistake: Companies can establish themselves as experts at exceeding expectations even without a legacy to back them up. Take RedEnvelope. Though founded in 1997 as 911gifts.com, RedEnvelope soon found its place in the constellation of superstar stores when veteran brand-shaper Hilary Billings came aboard in 1999 and transformed it into a high-end gifting company faster than you can lick a stamp. The company's attention to detail in everything from product selection to site design, combined with its exceptional customer service (which Billings takes very, very seriously) and wonderful packaging has gained it a reputation as one of the premier gift destinations on or off the Web.

While customers have come to expect that their expectations will be met, and often exceeded, by luxury brands and high-end companies, any company, no matter how small, or how relatively inexpensive its offering, can find ways to shoot for the moon and win its customers' hearts and loyalties in the process.

❋ REDENVELOPE: SEALING THE DEAL WITH CUSTOMERS

More often than not it seems that the joy of gift-giving gets undermined by the chore of gift-buying and gift-wrapping, and often, gift-delivering. After enduring this typically stressful and time-consuming process, we are often so relieved to hand the package over and cross it off our to-do lists that we forget to stop and enjoy the simple pleasures of giving gifts. That's why high-end retailer RedEnvelope is trying to change the way we experience the stress of giving, doing so by restoring deeper meaning and emotion to the art of giving.

Its name borrowed from the Asian tradition of giving gifts in small red envelopes, and its eclectic collection of gifts perfect for any occasion or no occasion at all, RedEnvelope is using modern, innovative means to reintroduce consumers to one of humanity's oldest traditions. And in the process it hopes to create an experience that exceeds everyone's expectations.

Though born during the late-nineties dot-com madness, RedEnvelope did not succumb to the gratuitous (and ultimately self-defeating) giveaways of its now-defunct peers, thanks in part to Chairman and Chief Marketing Officer Hilary Billings, who understands the difference between excessive hype and exceptional giving.

"Overdelivery is when you exceed customers' expectations with the purchase that they have made. If the quality of the product exceeds the expectations, if the delivery exceeds the expectations, if the experience in talking with the customer-service team exceeds the expectations, that is overdelivery," says Billings. "I've always felt that if a company paid a lot more attention to the quality of the experience that was at the core of what their business represented, they would have to do a lot less of that to maintain their customers."

A relative newcomer, RedEnvelope arrived just in time to help well-intentioned, time-starved consumers with their gifting needs. While the Web site and catalog are transforming the experience of gift-giving, Billings is developing a collection of "just because" gifts to inspire a revolution in the way Americans think about giving gifts.

The act of buying a gift through RedEnvelope is as special as the delight of receiving a gift someone had sent from them. RedEnvelope sparks imaginative giving by recommending products by lifestyle and personality ("the spa seeker," "the romantic") as well as by the more typical designations of gender, age, and occasion. Express and Corporate Gift sections make it easy for fast spenders and business givers, respectively, to get in and get out fast, but with just the right gift. And on the receiving end, the beautiful red box, tied with a cream-colored fabric ribbon, makes the moment special even before the recipient lifts the lid to discover the treasure inside.

"Generally, the whole gift market has been unsatisfying to consumers. There's this sort of dozen-roses-and-box-of-chocolates problem," Billings laments, looking at the way in which Americans typically view the obligation of gift-giving.

"But if you really look around the world, gift-giving tends to be much more spontaneous. It doesn't hover around holidays that have lots of pressure associated with them. Our hope in developing this brand was that Americans would grow to enjoy the wonderful benefits of the gift-giving experience, the way that many cultures around the world do today."

Often it's the little things that mean a lot to consumers, especially if they're a part of everyday experiences that usually don't stand out as exceptional. Sometimes it can be as simple as turning back the clock to a lost tradition by, say, giving a regular customer a "baker's dozen" (13 instead of 12) rolls when she stops by on her way home from work. Once considered a standard, few bakers these days even know what a baker's dozen is, much less offer that simple, old-fashioned extra to their customers.

Or an event of everyday exception can come in the form of an uncommonly nice courtesy, such as a postal carrier covering your packages in plastic on a rainy day so they don't get drenched on your doorstep before you return. These are the things that make consumers pause, smile, and reflect on what a pleasant surprise it is to be treated so well.

Relevance is also of great importance. To exceed customers' expectations, you first have to understand them. So don't rely on excessive marketing, packaging, or hype to exceed expectations. There's enough razzle-dazzle out there already without companies adding to the disco-ball atmosphere, so be mindful of the fact that consumers won't be impressed by a flashy email campaign unless its promoting a solid product with real value. Otherwise, you run the risk of setting up false expectations. It's the genuine gestures, the personal touches, the extra care that counts, not how much money you spend on celebrity endorsements or golf tournament sponsorships.

Superstar spokespeople may catch people's attention and build hype for a product in the short term, and they may be of value when used with relevance (and not overexposed) as inspirational role models whose prestige can reflect favorably on your brand. But at the end of the day, they're just the messengers for your company. They can't improve your service, your products, or your experience; they can only tell the world about them. As with everything else, it's quality that counts, above all.

> PEOPLE ARE . . . WILLING TO SPEND MONEY ON SOMETHING THAT IS TRUE, DURABLE, AND LASTING.
>
> **Rebecca Kotch, House of Blues**

Rebecca Kotch, Vice President of Retail for House of Blues, agrees. "I think value is something that people are looking for," she says. "People are really more cautious about where they're going to spend their money these days. But they're willing to spend money on something that is true, durable, and lasting." Which is why, Kotch says, House of Blues retail is going to branch out into a higher end of merchandise—fine art works—that have more longevity for purchasers than, say, mass-produced posters or souvenir *tchotchkes*. "Forget all that frivolous stuff that you're going to throw out in a year," Kotch says. Concentrate on the things that bring value and meaning to people's lives over time.

When you're thinking of handing out a goodie, remember that everyday giveaways like calendars, mouse-pads, and magnets, or even pens or T-shirts, may not have as much impact as items that relate directly to your consumers' lives or businesses. Which means that if you want people to advertise for your company by flashing your logo around, think seriously about what you're putting it on. Handing out cheesy or easily broken knickknacks emblazoned with your logo could have an opposite effect from the one you intended, if recipients dwell on the lack of quality instead of your company's generosity.

So take the time needed to explore extras or bonuses that would have the most meaning to your customers, and (if your logo is attached) will have the most likelihood of being seen—in a positive light—by their friends and associates. Perhaps you will choose to add free baseball caps, for the Little League team that orders its customized jerseys from your sports apparel shop; or to present a beautifully wrapped, branded rattle, when a mother-to-be registers for her baby shower at your boutique; or to give someone a chance to have a percentage of their purchase donated in their name to the charity of their choice. Whatever you do to exceed expectations, making it meaningful makes it better.

✳ THE VOICE OF THE CUSTOMER
SURPRISE ME WITH EXTRAS.

Okay, so I sound like I'm talking out of both sides of my mouth. Fickle, no. Complex, yes. I'm not interested in collecting more junk, but who doesn't enjoy a little surprise? I'm delighted when you give me something that I just didn't expect. Something unique, something special. When that happens, I tend to talk about it. And I know how you like that!

Here's how to take me by surprise. . . .

- **More than a greeting.** I love it when I walk in and you not only say hello but also give me a special insider's deal. Like when Victoria's Secret offered me $5 off any purchase simply for trying on a Body by Victoria bra. Indeed, I got excited not only by that little, unexpected bonus but also by the extra customer-service attention in helping me to find the perfect fit. (Did I buy the bra? But of course!) Sometimes just a small, on-the-spot incentive can go a long way toward jumpstarting my spending.

- **Packaged to please.** Wouldn't it be a pleasant surprise if a bag of potato chips could defy the infamous "contents will settle during shipment" disclaimer and be full when you opened it? Everyone likes getting more of something. That's why I love family-sized bottles of shampoo and lotion. But that doesn't mean I want or need a "superspecial deal" on a ten-gallon tub of popcorn and a bucket of soda when I go to the movies. So don't push me to buy ridiculously ungainly products I don't want or need.

■ **Timing is everything.** Nobody likes to wait in line to pay. And waiting while the sales associate struggles with a price-check, reloads the cash-register tape, or processes a credit is as annoying as it is tolerable. That's why Target blew me away recently. When the new-cash register technology they had installed crashed three times, requiring my $100 order to be rescanned again and again, the store manager rushed to my rescue before I could blow a fuse. He apologized for the technical difficulty, promised it would be short-lived, and offered a $3.00 discount coupon off my purchase that day or any day thereafter. His good timing made a bad situation not bad at all.

Likewise, customers will feel like they've been given special treatment when a customer-service representative goes out on a limb to offer assistance in finding a product, extending a special offer a few days past the deadline, or handling a unique request.

This is especially important for customers who interact with call-center or Web service associates. Sure, such indirect contacts can seem a bit distant and even impersonal; but when that invisible call-center rep tries a bit harder by hunting down a dress from an earlier catalog, or turns around a birthday gift to a nephew in record time, a customer will feel that company is really there for her.

TARGET—BE THEIR GUEST

While values abound at Target stores, shopping there is not your typical bargain-hunting adventure. Style isn't sacrificed to price, yet great deals are readily available—and without the seemingly requisite digging through bargain bins. Not even service is surrendered for the sake of a buck: Friendly, red-shirted associates treat customers like the "guests" they are and are highly visible throughout the store, while courtesy phones and price-checking gadgets are never more than an aisle or two away for those who prefer to help themselves.

Even the checkout experience takes Target out of the discount-store mix. Rather than letting guests linger in long lines, to ponder whether the shopping experience was worth the time it took just to pay for their goods, Target keeps most if not all of its registers open and running.

At first glance Target may look like a typical big-box discount store, with its aisles upon aisles of clothing and housewares, its toys and sporting goods, its snack foods and toiletries. But look a little closer and you'll discover that the store brands have a flair that goes way beyond the ordinary.

While some big discounters tag their apparel and household lines to TV stars and supermodels, Target has taken a more meaningful creative path by selecting some of the freshest and most renowned designers and creators to develop its product lines. From its affordable but stylish Michael Graves–designed household goods, to its dashing apparel by Mossimo Giannulli and its sleek, colorful cosmetics from makeup artist Sonia Kashuk, the message it sends out loud and clear to its customers is that Target is far from the low-rent district.

Maybe that's why so many of its loyal customers (many of whom are upscale consumers who might not normally frequent a discount store) have adopted the tongue-in-cheek pronunciation of "Targét"—because saying the store's name with a French accent somehow makes it seem even classier. Target's consistently creative approach shows that exceeding expectations is as much about finding new ways to do things better as it is about doing them better to begin with.

Even the most seemingly common courtesies matter, and the mere fact that they take place can exceed consumer expectations. If people have to wait in line for more than ten minutes, hand them a discount coupon for their next purchase. When they check out at the register, train the sales associate to make eye contact and offer a warm "Thanks so much for shopping with us." It may seem trivial, but for people who have become numbed by long lines or surly service, these brief flashes of warmth and humanity strike a chord that may resonate as a sense of fulfillment, no matter how minor they may seem at the time.

THE VOICE OF THE CUSTOMER
UNCOMMON COURTESIES.

Friendly goes a long way. It's amazing. When you're warm, pleasant, and helpful, it makes all the difference in how I think of you and your company. If you're snooty, lazy, or indifferent, that's a big turn-off, one that tells me you don't care. Turn on the charm, dial up the sincerity, and win me over.

Here's how to be as nice as your grandmother taught you to be. . . .

- **Apologies do count.** Mistakes happen, probably more than I want and certainly more than you realize. And that's okay, because we're all human. What's not okay is failing to take responsibility when you mess up. Long waits, late orders, poor quality—hey, it happens. But when it does, please say those simple words, "I'm sorry." Even if it isn't entirely your responsibility. Show some genuine empathy for my situation and I'll feel understood and inclined to forgive and forget, especially if you make amends along with the apology.

- **Be quick to make the fix.** Yes, an apology will tend to soothe my frustration. But don't forget to actually correct the problem as soon as possible. Know who is to be called for every conceivable customer issue, and have those numbers ready for me when I call. Better yet, give everyone who deals with me the power to make things right for me: to take a return, make an exchange, offer a refund or an upgrade. I know I hate having to ask, "Can I speak to your manager?" as much as I bet you hate hearing it, so why not spare us both the hassle?

Think of this game of exceeding customer expectations as competing in a pole-vaulting event. Once you've cleared the first bar, you know it will continue to be raised—by your competitors as well as by your customers. And if you're really at the top of your game you'll be raising it yourself, so as to continue challenging your personal best. And that means you've got to stay in training to continue winning over customers by showing them that your company has the stamina, the will, and the imagination to clear even the highest bar and to take your customers with you as you soar ever higher.

DEMANDMENT 08: **EXCEED MY EXPECTATIONS—SELF-EVALUATION**

Now that you've read this Demandment, see how you stack up. The checkpoints in this form reflect the key takeaways from the "Voice of the Customer" sections. Identify where your company could stand some improvement, and you'll have a shot at building bridges with the people who keep you in business.

8. PUT ME IN CHARGE	Excellent	Good	Poor
Over-compensate.	Services and features are in place, to make up for channel or competitive deficiencies or weaknesses.	Concerns over channel or competitive deficiencies and other weaknesses are addressed when consumers report them.	Unresponsive to consumer concerns over channel or competitive deficiencies and other weaknesses.
Do more than you should.	Overdelivery is a shared philosophy that empowers the front lines in the company.	Overdelivery is important in special circumstances.	Overdelivery is a consideration only after everything else has been taken care of.
Surprise me with extras.	Extras are designed to delight consumers even when things went right.	Extras designed to appease/please consumers when something has gone wrong.	Extras are not part of the program.
Uncommon courtesies.	Employees willingly extend apologies, and have definitive guidelines/allow-ances for satisfying a customer on the spot.	Employees extend apologies and have definitive guidelines for making amends.	Employees do not have definitive guidelines for making amends.

09

The Ninth Demandment

reward me

WHAT HAVE YOU DONE FOR ME LATELY? It's a universal question asked by consumers who expect companies to give something special back in exchange for their loyalty. Companies that deliver exceptional experiences earn loyalty by doing so consistently over time. But those shooting for the ultimate in customer commitment—the long-term kind—can't stop at the actual experience. They have to think about how to make their consumers feel exceptionally valued even after they walk out the door with a full shopping bag. That's where rewards come in.

Rewards come in many shapes and sizes: from the prize in the cereal box that kids will dive in up to their elbows to retrieve, to the family vacation earned in frequent-flier miles after many a business trip by mom or dad. And while these bonuses may not be the primary reason somebody shops in a certain store, stays at a particular hotel, or buys a specific brand of gasoline, pleasant perks can certainly help sweeten the incentive to choose one brand over another.

In a world where brands blur together amid an indistinguishable array of stores and catalogs, experiences and offerings, the tipping point of differentiation to induce customer loyalty may be a well-designed shopping-points program, meaningful freebies, or other powerful perks.

So loosen the ribbons and slip off the bows, because it's time to unwrap the Ninth Demandment: **Reward Me.** Consumers aren't standing in front of you looking for a handout—but they do have their hand out for you, waiting for it to be held as a sign of personal service, expecting it to be filled with special treats, or hoping to be given the keys to a kingdom of exclusive events. Those outstretched hands are seeking assurance that you value them, and waiting for evidence that you care enough to reward them for being your customer.

> "REWARD ME" IS, IN SOME WAYS, A CODE FOR "APPRECIATE ME."

Rewarding customers is about more than giving them free stuff or 10 percent off on their next purchase—it's about acknowledgment of what they mean to your company. **Reward Me** is, in some ways, a code for "Appreciate Me." We're not talking about staging a hokey series of "customer appreciation" day sales, which tend to be just like every other kind of sale, directed at anyone who walks in the door with money in their pocket. Nope, we're talking about sending a clear, meaningful message to customers who may feel less than cared for or cared about these days. When a company shows its gratitude to customers through truly rewarding loyalty programs, invitations to elite events, service upgrades, or other special perks, they're wooing customers in all the right ways.

✳ THE VOICE OF THE CUSTOMER
ACKNOWLEDGE MY VALUE.

I spend and I spend and I spend with you. And what do I get in return? A smile at the checkout? That's nice, but I want more. I want to feel appreciated—and not just because I just bought something with you, but because I've been buying from you all along. I need to know that my business matters beyond the money you've made from me. Acknowledge my value by telling me that I'm one of your best customers— and by showing how much you appreciate me.

Here's how to show you care. . . .

■ **Know enough to know who I am.** The worst thing is when I'm a regular—a big spender—completely and utterly loyal, but you haven't go a clue. You don't have any records of my purchases, and don't know how often I shop at your store. So you treat me just like everybody else. I'm not asking for preferential treatment: I don't want to get ahead of someone else in line, or anything like that. I just want you recognize that I'm really, really important to you.

■ **A gift of thanks.** You don't have to have a big fancy program to convince me I'm worthwhile. I like the way BP handles it. They track my gasoline purchases, and then periodically send a simple thank-you letter and enclose a $20 cash card for free gasoline. It doesn't even cover the cost of a fill-up in these days of gas-guzzling SUVs, but it's a genuine, tangible, even predictable reward. And it somehow creates a friendly appeal for an otherwise faceless company.

Of course, there are plenty of wrong ways to try to earn people's business: through false rewards, bait-and-switch offers, or meaningless membership clubs. And because loyalty programs can be costly to develop, market, and maintain, companies find themselves walking a razor-thin line that divides retention value from program costs. One of the worst ways to earn long-term loyalty is to trade rewards up-front for a long-term contract (as cellular phone companies do)—they may be locking customers in for the short term, but they're training them to see their commitments as limited-term engagements, bound by contracts but little else.

The path to satisfying the **Reward Me** demands of your customers is paved throughout the other demandments in this book. Because rewards are meaningless unless they have value, you have to understand what your customers' values are: what they need, want, and care about (**Get to Know Me**). You have to make loyalty programs simple to sign up for, access, understand, and use (**Make It Easy, Guide Me,** and **24/7**). To further reward upper-tier customers (that supremely loyal 20 percent who provide 80 percent of your sales), you may want to go even farther, offering greater control over reward selections (**Put Me in Charge**) and pampering them with VIP events and special treatment (**Exceed My Expectations**) to help retain and expand their devotion. Nail these concepts, and rewarding your customers will be a natural part of the evolution of your relationship.

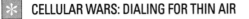 CELLULAR WARS: DIALING FOR THIN AIR

While reward programs often drive customer loyalty, head-on competition, when taken to an extreme, can lead to less-than-rewarding warfare scenarios. Grocery stores, gas stations, and video-rental stores are among the busiest beavers in the loyalty game, and so, in any given town, they are likely to be competing against similar programs at every turn.

Companies that try to undercut each other's programs by offering freebies, but without locking in customer loyalty in some other way at the same time, are asking for the same kinds of problems that have led to airfare wars (in which carriers often lost their shirts, or at least their seats, by trying to knock each other out of hot markets via offers of ridiculously low, loss-leader fares).

The cellular industry has gotten caught up in an ever-escalating reward war that's led to giveaways of everything from gadgety phones to eons worth of weekend minutes. On the upside, most of these freebies are tied to annual contracts (the longer the contract, the more freebies offered up-front). So the costs of retention and acquisition are smartly aligned. Plus, while the gear may be expensive to hand out, the "cost" of giving away free airtime is approximately the same as giving away free air, since airtime minutes are an elastic, invisible commodity that cost nothing to produce and are rarely if ever used to the full capacity of the giveaway. Companies still have to foot the bill for their network infrastructure and customer-service and -support systems, but those would need to be built and maintained for the growing cellular population no matter how many free airtime minutes fly out the kiosk door.

On the down side, customers have become almost Pavlovian in their response to the cell wars, salivating in the expectation that a bigger, better cellular deal is just around the corner. Because of the industry's rabid competition for customers—especially in emerging markets where a fresh audience of uncontracted consumers awaits—many potential customers (especially those not driven by a specific need) simply sit back and wait for an even more incredible deal to surface before they sign up. So up and up the offers go, with companies practically bidding against themselves for new customer contracts.

Is warfare always a bad thing, when it comes to loyalty programs? Not if the customer wins out, and the company can bear the burden. But if escalation takes all the meaning out of the reward, as companies engage in "Top this!" behavior, their customers will either sit on the sidelines or, more likely, play both sides. Enticing customers to become mercenary double agents is no way to win a war, or their ultimate loyalty.

Still, there is a way for everyone to win, and it's all about longevity. Cellular companies should stop thinking of their customer relationships as being expiration-dated. After all, wireless communications will be around for a while. So rather than trying to woo customers into a contract that offers a lot up-front and nothing in the middle, why not start thinking about the longer-term: Give them better value, better service, and better-quality products throughout the duration of their contract, and reward them in ways big and small throughout that time, with surprise perks like a free month of wireless Web service. When consumers begin to feel committed to their wireless companies out of loyalty opposed to contractual obligation, then everyone will be a winner.

With more than half of the grocery stores, and nearly a quarter of the retail apparel stores in the United States (not to mention virtually every major airline, hotel chain, and rental car company) offering membership clubs, frequent-buyer cards, or other perky plans, a loyalty program in and of itself isn't much of a point of differentiation. That is, unless you use it as a way to extend your relationship with customers by serving their needs at a fundamental level, rather than simply offering generic rewards or discounts.

That's what the Green Hills Grocery Story in Syracuse, N.Y., has done. They've figured out how to crack the code of customer loyalty by rewarding customers—their *best* customers—with incentives that go far beyond the norm. This small, 68-year-old family-owned and -operated store is hardly in the league of the big food chains, but its Mom- and Pop-intimacy with its customers allows it to get to the heart of the matter and to give from the heart as well.

The idea is so simple it's brilliant: Green Hills rewards customers who spend $100 a week, week in and week out, with "Diamond" status in its membership program. Diamond members not only get the standard free turkey at Thanksgiving (fresh, not frozen); the Hawkins family (which runs Green Hills) also gives Diamond members a free, hand-selected 7-foot fir tree during the holidays. And the perks keep percolating year-round, with special offers, great freebies, and major savings coupons all proving that the store is as committed to its customers as its customers are to the store. When a flood left the area without electricity in 1986, the store even sent its Diamond members a letter of concern and a savings coupon, to help replace the food lost when their refrigerators stopped chilling out. Such thoughtful, relevant rewards add up to a sense of community and caring that makes it easy for families to bypass other grocery stores and other loyalty programs.

Green Hills' rewardingly relevant approach offers a lesson for any company trying to cut through the charm braceletlike clutter of plastic membership tags that dangle by the dozens from consumer key chains. Since keeping customers focused and loyal to one loyalty program (and thus, one store) over another is tricky at best, companies must find more compelling ways to woo customers into a longer-term relationship, and offer more meaningful rewards for their best customers.

Companies get more than loyalty in return for successful rewards programs: They also collect valuable data about their customers. But you can't be collecting it without giving something of greater value back. And the more you take from consumers—not just in money, but in information they choose to share—the more you should be prepared to give back to them, in the form of better experiences that serve their needs.

According to a study done in 2000 by McKinsey Co., 70 percent of consumers who belong to grocery-store loyalty programs, and 79 percent of those who belong to retail apparel programs, say they still actively seek alternatives to the stores where they receive loyalty rewards. So points alone aren't the point: There's got to be a strong perceived value in the membership experience that makes people eager to stay loyal as they earn greater and greater rewards.

THE VOICE OF THE CUSTOMER
MAKE MEMBERSHIP MEANINGFUL.

Don't ask me to sign up just because you want to collect my info. I know it's tempting, but I'll see right through you if you lure me in with big promises for unique services, personalized content, privileged access, or special offers—and then, when I try to visit the clubhouse, there's nobody home. Even if you charge me a small fee I'm okay with that, if I get something of value on a consistent and predictable basis. But I gotta get something back, big time, or the only thing you'll be tracking about me is when I stopped buying from you.

The loyalty game isn't an even match when it comes to industries; companies that sell products instead of services end up taking a bigger hit for program costs, because they pay out of pocket for whatever they give away. The greatest loss leaders are loyalty programs that try to do too much too soon for too many customers, blurring the program's purpose by targeting both sides of the fence—acquisition and retention—with equal gusto.

Companies that offer faster rewards in the form of premium merchandise or deep discounts will usually take losses on all but their most loyal (20 percent) customers. And that loyal royalty often ends up subsidizing the costs of the membership perks for program-hopping shoppers who are uninspired to make a greater commitment by becoming more frequent patrons, since they can get similar, low-level rewards at so many other stores.

Sure, you could get your customers to pay directly for the privileges that come with membership, and in some cases that model has merit—especially when purchasers who make a small investment receive high-quality communications and frequent discounts or rewards in exchange for the up-front payment. It's perhaps less rewarding in the purest sense of the word, but fee-based programs have proven effective with shoppers who return again and again to "get their money's worth" out of a premiere video club (such as Blockbuster's) or bookstore membership once they've paid for it.

Unlike retail or grocery, where the costs of fulfilling loyalty programs can outweigh the benefits of customer retention, sectors such as travel and tourism have traditionally succeeded at keeping program costs down while increasing customer loyalty. The reason? They deal in "perishable" goods that are lost forever if not sold in a short period of time. Once a plane takes off or another night passes into day, the airline or hotel has lost the chance to earn any money on empty seats or empty rooms. Thus, it doesn't really cost much to give away free flights or free nights (or to offer first class or suite upgrades) when those same seats or rooms would have gone unused anyway.

Even companies that sell merchandise instead of services can take a cue from the airline and hotel industries by treating customers to upgrades and perks instead of products. From personal shoppers to extended shopping hours, exclusive member lounges, behind-the-scenes tours, or members-only Web-site features, giving customers the VIP treatment can be a smart way to keep them happy without the gifts or gimmicks.

THE VOICE OF THE CUSTOMER
ROLL OUT THE RED CARPET.

I love the VIP treatment. Who doesn't? If I'm a frequent flier, a mobile-phone warrior, a shoe fanatic, or a carryout devotee, I expect something more from you. Treat me with the best service you have, and I'll be hooked.

Here's how to pile it on. . . .

■ **Upgrade my service.** Maybe a red carpet is overkill, but an upgrade will do just fine, thank you very much. A better seat, more attentive service by phone, email, or in person, more channels or options or additional minutes. Whatever you usually offer, please up it for me—on your dime, this time.

■ **Include me in special events.** Invite me to something I can't otherwise attend. Not just to sideshows that don't matter to your business or to me, but to something of value. I'm talking preview sales or trunk shows, performances, product reviews, online forums, or gala openings. When I'm invited I know I'm important, and when I attend, I feel important.

■ **Make events more special.** Once you've lured me in, don't blow it. Too many companies attempt to pull out the stops over the holidays only to be lost in the shuffle of every other company trying to capture my attention and devotion. Some waste a perfectly good schmoozing opportunity by serving stale chips and tasteless, mass-produced cookies. Don't fall victim to the holiday blues. Find your own time of year, make it festive for me, and do it up right.

It should come as no surprise that the airline industry innovated the modern loyalty program. American Airlines introduced the first frequent-flier program in 1981—created by the company's president to recapture the kinds of consumer loyalty once sparked by S & H Green Stamps. The program was so successful that today every major airline, hotel, and rental-car company offers a membership program for regular customers.

Yet, for all the mileage points and perks handed out in the past two decades, companies rarely have to bear the full weight of delivering on their promotional reward offers. This is particularly true in the realm of frequent flier-mileage programs. It's estimated that as many as 3 trillion frequent-flier miles have yet to be redeemed by their recipients—in part because (at least until the post-9/11 downturn in the travel industry) it's been a lot easier to earn points than to redeem them, what with blackout periods, the small number of program seats available per flight, and other limitations on redemption.

So while frequent fliers watch their mileage points rack up, their sense of having been rewarded by—or feeling loyal to—a particular airline may not be as high-flying. With so many miles in their accounts but so few opportunities to spend them (unless they can be transferred to a broader program, such as American Express Membership Miles), consumers may look at their frequent-flier miles as something akin to those thousands of free weekend airtime minutes they got with their cellular phones. Yes, they have them, but do they ever expect to use them all? Not a chance—unless the airline encourages them to donate the miles to charity. It doesn't help that so many airlines still expire their miles after a certain number of years, which only adds to a member's sense of futility about even being able to use them before he loses them.

And even if a consumer knows he'll eventually get something for all those points, how do loyalty programs that take a long time to accrue enough value for worthwhile reward gain any foothold among those customers who prefer more immediate gratification? One way

✳ MEGA-HERTZ: WHERE MEMBERSHIP IS GOLDEN

Back in 1989, when Hertz introduced the first members-only loyalty program in the rental-car industry, the company set a gold standard for road-warrior loyalty programs by doing more than letting customers earn points toward rewards. It also set about significantly improving the car-renting experience for its most loyal "Gold" members, the business travelers who demand faster and easier ways to get around and get back to work.

Hertz's #1 Club Gold program—for its best customers—has innovated such now-standard practices as membership profiles for faster rental, advance contract generation (so members can go straight to the car and bypass the lines at the counter), and dedicated customer support. And there's just something about stepping off a bus and seeing your name up in lights (even if it's just directing you to your car's parking space) that makes you feel a little special.

Thus this program has set a gold standard for competitors to try to match, and many have done so with some success. Still, Hertz #1 Club remains the #1 rental-car loyalty program in the world, despite its fee-based membership. With Hertz's locations at 45 airports around the country, frequent business travelers have become loyal Hertz club members, in part because of the sheer ease of the process.

One of the company's smartest innovations has been the GEM (Gold Electronic Manifest) system, which allows shuttle-bus drivers to collect the names of renters as they board the bus, then transmit that information via a wireless device to the rental location. By the time the customer arrives at the Hertz location, associates already have prepped the car for a fast escape (right down to the popped trunk, ready for luggage). All the customer has to do is step off the bus, find his name on the electronic board, and head straight to his car.

To the #1 Gold member, it's a seamless, queue-less process. For Hertz, the fact that its club members have the fastest possible way to get from airport to open road, with the fewest stops or waits in between, is its greatest accomplishment. Seeing less of their best customers is the whole point of this rewarding program.

is by dangling the prize in front of the consumer on a regular basis, and by offering escalating levels of rewards that allow people to get a little something faster, or to save up for the big prize later on.

That's how the American Express Membership Miles program works: Whether you want to redeem a small number of miles for a package of bagels, or a truckload for a trip around the world, it's up to members to choose how many, or how few, of their miles to spend. Since the miles don't expire, there's less of a panic to use them. And since the rewards get exponentially more enticing the higher you go, the incentive to keep spending money and earning points toward bigger and better rewards is built into the system. And while American Express charges a fee for membership in its program, its miles never expire.

Multiple-partner programs like American Express's are one way to get people earning, accruing, and using their points in ways that build loyalty and inspire program affinity. The remarkably successful

Air Miles program in Canada, which began in 1992, has signed up about 65 percent of Canadian households, and serves as a role model for many multiple-partner programs. The beauty of these programs is that no single-program partner bears the full burden of redeeming rewards, yet all are strengthened by the relationship with other premier partners.

✳ THE VOICE OF THE CUSTOMER
LET ME EARN IT THE OLD-FASHIONED WAY.

> While I'm all for instant gratification, I sometimes enjoy the build-up and satisfaction that comes with working toward a grand prize of my choosing. Collecting points, labels, or bottle caps for things that I routinely buy can be like a game—one that I'm destined to win if I just stay on track and you don't make me jump through too many hoops to get to my goal. Pampers gave me and my spouse a pretty good reason to keep buying their brand: We were madly saving up proofs of purchase for an irresistible, foot-powered Fisher-Price Jeep Junior for our son. Now, if I only can save up for the battery powered, ride-on Little Wrangler Enforcer!

But even companies that don't team up with other program partners can spread the love around by using cross-channel reward programs that can expose customers to new channels while giving them the convenience of earning and redeeming rewards online, in-store, or through a catalog. A lot of multichannel players are catching on—Hallmark's Gold Crown Card™ program even provides a separate, more personalized site for card-holders; and both the Sharper Image's Customer Rewards™ program and Staples Dividend$™ program let shoppers earn rewards wherever they spend with the brand. Likewise, Barnes and Noble's Reader's Advantage™ members receive a discount whether they shop online (5%) or in-store (10%).

Having a seamless, integrated reward program that follows a customer from channel to channel can also strengthen your relationships by showing your customers that you know and recognize them, and reward them as special customers no matter where they touch your brand.

✳ THE VOICE OF THE CUSTOMER
REWARD ME WHEREVER I GO.

> You have many places where I can buy from or talk to you, so don't limit my rewards to just your store, or just your catalog. Let me redeem in your store, by phone, or on the Web. This is a win/win situation, because when I'm not restricted to using rewards in a single place, it's more convenient for me. And then my purchases aren't likely to be restricted to a single place, either. Rewards that I can earn and use wherever I meet up with your brand show me you're one company, and that you see me as one customer worth having.

Loyalty-point programs are just one example of reward programs that give something back to customers. Sometimes the gift of giving can be such a powerful tool that companies see their loyalty rise by letting their members share the love with causes they care about or friends they want to pamper.

One trend that gained popularity about a decade ago has become an annual back-to-school ritual for many communities: collecting grocery-store register tapes and turning them in for student computers, books, and other school supplies and equipment. Other variations on this sort of community-support loyalty program include PTAs selling store "scrip" that raises money for the local schools, and fast-food restaurants dedicating proceeds from designated days or nights to local schools or other charities.

Along these same lines, Target has had great success in bolstering its image as a dedicated community partner through the Target Community Card. By donating 1 percent of card-holder purchases, Target makes buyers feel that they're doing something for their own community by shopping at the store.

Your customers are always your best salespeople, which is why rewarding them for spreading the word about your company to friends and family can drive your business in two directions at the same time: out into the world of new customers, and down deeper into the realm of loyal, referring customers.

Word of mouth has long been a staple of business success, but when the Internet came along the idea of viral marketing assumed epidemic proportions. Now, with a simple email campaign or online "tell-a-friend" form, companies can give their customers a way to pass along special offers to their pals.

And focused tell-a-friend reward campaigns can work just as well off-line. QPB (the Quality Paperback Book Club, part of the Book-of-the-Month Club family, which also uses these tactics) has expanded its loyal community of buyers and readers by asking them to pass along introductory membership deals to friends and families. For every pal who signs up, not only does that friend get a bunch of books for a buck, but the referring member also earns free books. QPB members also earn membership points for every book they buy (redeemable for more books, of course), and those rewards often are doubled for special purchases. When you read between the lines, it's a smart, on-brand loyalty program for avid readers.

✳ THE VOICE OF THE CUSTOMER
MAKE MY WORD OF MOUTH COUNT.

It's funny to think about how many choices I make, in a given day or week, about where to go and what to buy. The majority of those decisions are fueled by suggestions made to me by coworkers, friends, family, neighbors, etc. But so few companies are making it worth my while to pass along the good word about them to others. If you only realized it, I could be one of your best sales reps—and that's got to be worth something to you.

Here's how to get me on your sales team. . . .

- **Just ask me.** I can go through the list: hairdresser, cleaning lady, accountant, mortgage lender, life insurance agent, plumber, electrician, dentist, and physician. None has actually asked me to refer his or her services to a friend. Maybe they're too proud. Too busy. Or poor marketers. If they simply asked me to pass along their name and number, though, I might actually make the effort.

- **Sweeten the pot.** I like to help out my relatives, neighbors, and colleagues, don't get me wrong. But sometimes it's a little easier when there's something in it for me. Amazon does this by giving me a way to offer friends discounts on books I've just purchased that I think they might like; if they buy, I get a discount on my next purchase, too. This is a win for me and for my friends.

As mentioned in the Eighth Demandment, **Exceed My Expectations**, giveaways or gifts with purchases have long been a staple of the loyalty game, though they have to be relevant enough to stand out. Junkie freebies will probably sit unused in a drawer, attracting more dust than loyalty. But if you

JUNKIE FREEBIES WILL PROBABLY SIT UNUSED IN A DRAWER, ATTRACTING MORE DUST THAN LOYALTY.

reward your customers with gifts in the truest sense of the word—gifts of special services, sizable product samples, timely mementos (such as leather-bound desk calendars), or other pleasant surprises that stand out as thoughtful signs of appreciation—you'll avoid the bottom-of-the-drawer dumping ground where lesser bonuses end up.

THE VOICE OF THE CUSTOMER
GREAT GIFTS ARE GREAT REWARDS.

Let's face it, everybody loves a present. Especially when it's truly a surprise and something worth having. Forget the lousy coffee cups with bad graphics and corny sayings. They just add clutter to my cupboard full of misfit mugs. Give me something nice, something relevant, something I'd be glad to show off if given the chance.

Here's how to select my gift with care. . . .

■ **Become the object of my affection.** Don't put your name on anything you're not proud of, or somehow convinced I'll simply love to own. If it's not well designed and purposeful, or doesn't add value to my life, don't waste your money. You're doing more harm than good that way. So forget the acrylic key chains and ballpoint pens. You can't afford to be so out of touch.

■ **Wrap it up nicely.** Maybe it's shallow of me, but you know what? I actually do judge a book by its cover. And I judge a store or company by how nicely they present themselves, and how nicely their presents are presented. Banana Republic sends its best customers a token gift such as a leather picture frame artistically wrapped in vellum, ribbon, and modern graphics. The total package, not merely the gift, conveys a meaningful message of thanks. Mission accomplished.

- **Cash cards are king.** Money talks. And money, in the form of cash cards, walks as well. It walks me straight to the store to spend it along with my own money, too—which I'm sure is part of your grand plan. Those little plastic cash cards mailed out by the likes of Kohl's, Old Navy, The Gap, and others are hard to resist. They do much more than reward me, they invite me back into the store with a reason to spend. Who can resist, with a cash card in hand?

Identifying and rewarding your very best customers is another smart move, both in the short run and over the long haul. If they're so valuable to you, prove it to them by offering perks such as superior service with personal shoppers and free gift wrapping; special access to private sales and customer-appreciation events; or real discounts on every purchase, such as Chico's offers its Passport members after they reach a certain spending level. And give them special—regular—discount days to keep them coming back month in and month out, as GNC does with its "Super Tuesdays" program for Gold Card Members, who earn 10 percent off purchases made on the first Tuesday of the month. Garden Botanika's membership club offers similar savings, and adds in an extra saving during the member's birthday month.

Tiering can be tricky, of course: While you want your best customers to feel appreciated and aware of their special treatment, you don't want to have the customers who have yet to attain that level of significance feeling like second-class citizens. So don't flaunt a loyalty caste system, promote the added benefits given to higher-end customers and aspirational customers—much in the manner of cultural institutions or political organizations. Do this by subtly highlighting the value of membership in the inner circles of top patronage.

The value of rewards extends far beyond the dollar costs to a company. When rewards are done well, consumers feel appreciated for their loyalty. They know a company has recognized the importance of their business, and have a sense that the longer they stay with that company, the more they will be appreciated (and rewarded).

So why wait until your customers ask "What have you done for me lately?" when you could be answering that question every time they open their wallet and see that reward card, or whenever they earn a coupon after a minimum purchase because of their "best customer" status? The relationship you're seeking with customers has to be about more than money; it has to invoke in them the awareness of a gracious, grateful "Thank you" that lives on in their minds long after the cash-register drawer has closed.

DEMANDMENT 09: **REWARD ME—SELF-EVALUATION**

Now that you've read this Demandment, see how you stack up. The checkpoints in this form reflect the key takeaways from the "Voice of the Customer" sections. Identify where your company could stand some improvement, and you'll have a shot at building bridges with the people who keep you in business.

9. REWARD ME	Excellent	Good	Poor
Acknowledge my value.	Program in place to reward consumers for big or frequent purchases.	Occasionally reward consumers for big or frequent purchases.	No reward for high-spending shoppers.
Make membership meaningful.	Membership benefits are reliable, and program adds value to the relationship.	Membership program adds value to the relationship.	No clear value in membership.
Roll out the red carpet.	Consistently acknowledge consumer loyalty through a system of perks or upgrades.	Randomly acknowledge consumer loyalty with occasional perks and upgrades.	No acknowledgment of consumer loyalty.
Let me earn it the old-fashioned way.	Create tiered program that encourages and celebrates achievement.	Create tiered program of rewards.	No tiered reward program in place.
Reward me wherever I go.	Reward system is seamless across channels, and can be easily accessed by customers in all channels.	Reward system applies to all channels but can not be accessed by customers in all channels.	Reward system is channel-specific only.
Make my word of mouth count.	Consumers get perks from referring friends, and the friends get a perk or discount for first purchase.	Consumers get perks from referring friends.	Consumers don't get perks by referring friends.
Great gifts are great rewards.	Give consumers gifts that they perceive to be of high value.	Give consumers relevant gifts.	Giveways are neither relevant nor desirable.

The Tenth Demandment

stay with me

FOR RELATIONSHIPS TO STAND THE TEST OF TIME, they require nourishment, compassion, communication, and honesty. Staying committed means staying in touch between visits; following through on the promises you've made, even if you've both seen some changes over the years; and making sure that the other person knows you're there for them, every step of the way. And all of these elements are as relevant to the relationships companies hope to forge with their consumers as to those between individuals.

To retain and nurture consumer relationships, companies must pursue, promote, and promulgate a sense of commitment that not only transcends the transaction but that actually fills in the empty space between transactions.

That's how the two-way streets that carry customers back and forth to companies again and again are paved: by fixing the speed-bumps, filling in the potholes, and offering a safe and smooth transit across that great divide from interaction to interaction.

The Tenth Demandment—**Stay with Me**—closes the loop on the customer relationship and serves as the final chapter in this roadmap to meeting consumer demands, in large part because it's about follow-through, follow-up, and simply maintaining a following even during the quiet periods when companies and their consumers are apart. It's about fulfilling the short-term promises of the deal, and then keeping the lines of communication and awareness open during that quiet period. And it's about wrapping things up neatly and beautifully, even while setting the stage for further interactions— ending one cycle and beginning another.

The Ten Demandments are all about what companies must do to build and strengthen engaging, meaningful, useful, and trustworthy customer experiences. And while most of those tactics, touch-points, and techniques apply to the up-front period when consumers are actively engaged with a company or brand as they move along the path toward purchase or engagement, **Stay with Me** is about all the things that happen after the fact in the short term and in the long term that will eventually bring the consumer back to the beginning of the cycle.

That journey starts with consumer awareness of a need, service, or product, and travels along the road of decision support to the transaction and—companies hope—the immediate satisfaction of having had a good experience. But to take consumers to the greatest level of loyalty and delight you must lift them up to the next level, elevating their experience with you from mere satisfaction to a long-lasting gratification that translates into loyalty to your brand, products, and experience.

In some ways, **Stay with Me** is the most difficult of the Demandments. It's the most open-ended, and the least defined in terms of specific time-periods, traditional tactics, and experience-drivers. Yet it's one of the most critical elements for success, because it's all about retention.

Research from the *Harvard Business Review,* the Gartner Group, and others shows that acquiring a new customer can cost as much as 30 to 40 percent more than retaining an existing one. That means that improving retention rates by only 5 percent can increase profitability to the tune of 25 to 50 percent. Retain even more customers, and the profits increase accordingly. *You* do the math!

Retention means keeping consumers inside the loyalty loop for as long as possible. To get your customers to stay with you, you've got to find ways to stay with them as they travel the continuum that carries them in a closed circuit through the "before," "during," and "after" stages of their need for your services, expertise, or products. And getting consumers to stay with your brand through repeated cycles means keeping your brand experience in their mind during the time when "after" slowly morphs into "before" once more, as the process begins anew. That's the loyalty loop that leads to long-term relationships with consumers.

RETENTION MEANS KEEPING CUSTOMERS INSIDE THE LOYALTY LOOP AS LONG AS POSSIBLE.

And it's really a two-part process: handling the short-term details of the post-purchase phase, and then extending the relationship into the quiet period that follows. Getting the post-purchase experience right is like a short sprint at the start of a much longer race for customer loyalty. And if you trip and fall out of the starting gate, you're unlikely to get a customer to run a marathon alongside you.

✳ THE VOICE OF THE CUSTOMER
IT'S NOT OVER 'TIL IT'S OVER.

You may have my money but not my satisfaction. Which is worth more to you? It's frustrating for me when I get home and discover that your product doesn't work as you had promised, that it's more difficult to install, or that it's the wrong fit, color, or answer to my problem. And yes, I know, it's probably my fault, not yours. I may have picked up the wrong product, misread the package, or opted to try it on at home. But regardless, if it's not right, you should be ready to make it right. Open your arms and your policies to let me return it for a refund or exchange so that the last leg of our transaction is a pleasant one.

Here's how to seal our deal with integrity. . . .

■ **Provide reassurance.** Tell me I made a good decision, when I'm paying or soon after. Seriously. That makes me feel good, especially if I'm the type who's prone to second thoughts. And third thoughts. And if I have to wait for my purchase, make sure I know when it will arrive and ensure that it does so on time and well protected. Throw in a little fanfare when I open the package, to make up for the delay. Build my confidence, and you'll keep my business.

Make my returns hassle-free. Tell me your return or exchange policy at the register, on my receipt, and on your site. It's only fair that I have to hang on to my receipt, but spare me your 10-day return policy. Give me at least 30 days—though I know I can't be wearing your ball gown to a month of galas and then bring it back in tatters! Let me make my return by mail or at your store, no matter where I made my purchase. Be courteous and process my return quickly, without calling for assistance from a supervisor. Or better yet, save me a trip and let me call to arrange for a pick-up at my convenience. Now that's hassle-free.

- **Make it easier to return gifts.** Everybody loves a gift. And a gift receipt. I know that the person I gave it to can return the gift without having the price I paid for it staring up at them from the register receipt; and I may never have to know they decided to return it. But when I try to give gifts online, things seem to fall apart. If someone returns a gift I sent them on the Web, my account ends up being credited as if I were the one who made the return. So then I have to find another gift, and we both have to face the embarrassment of knowing that my original gift wasn't well received. *Ick!* So please, take a tip from the folks at Sears, Old Navy, and other stores that give me gift receipts: Don't turn *my* gift into *your* goof.

- **Credit my account promptly.** If I don't want an exchange, I expect you to credit my account right away. It's easier in stores, where I can hand over the card I originally made the charge on and get the credit back right then and there. But I get nervous about how this works online. So I appreciate it when CDNow emails me, after they've given me credit for an online return. Don't make me wonder if you've done your job; I already feel resigned to double-checking my monthly statement just to be sure. And it's a

> good thing I do: I've had months go by without proper
> crediting to my account, which make me think that those
> companies are either unorganized, greedy, or both. Give
> credit where credit is due, and *when* it's due.

No matter how much great work you've done to move a consumer happily through the decision phase to the transaction or commitment, things can crumble after the fact owing to a bad return or exchange experience, fulfillment failure, poor complaint resolution, or other missteps that sour an otherwise good experience in a consumer's mind and memory.

The stakes are particularly high for companies that sell through e-commerce channels, where people often are buying more on faith than on tactile exploration. With less opportunity to touch, feel, or otherwise experience products or services before the purchase, e-commerce buyers are at a disadvantage going into the transaction.

That's likely one reason why, in the year 2000, McKinsey & Co. reported that almost 25 percent of the products purchased online were returned—a number that jumped to 35 percent for apparel purchases. A similar 2000 study conducted by Pricewaterhouse-Coopers revealed that 29 percent of Internet shoppers had returned merchandise purchased online at least once; the most frequent reason given for returns was that the products failed to meet their expectations. In addition, the report noted that 41 percent of online shoppers had wanted to return items, but chose not to because they thought it would be too much of a hassle.

But according to McKinsey, dissatisfaction with products is only a part of the problem: The research-and-strategy firm estimated that making good on fulfillment mistakes cost e-commerce companies some $2.5 *billion* in 2000.

Fulfillment is more than box-deep; it's a word that resonates not only with companies that want to accurately ful-

FULFILLMENT IS MORE THAN BOX-DEEP.

fill orders but also with consumers who expect—now, demand—to feel fulfilled by their interactions with the companies to which they are loyal. All the more reason to give people the best possible experience when the box arrives at the door, from the moment they recognize your brand name on the package and anticipate the contents, to the instant they lift the merchandise out and see how wonderfully it meets their expectations and fulfills their needs.

These emotions are magnified when ordering gifts. While the Internet and catalog shopping have made gift-giving easier in many ways, giving us access to a vast selection of products and providing us with the ease of shipping and delivery handled from afar, givers no longer have the ability to hand-select, wrap, and package the gift themselves. So when they entrust a company with fulfilling a gift order, they're also entrusting them with getting it right, and, in essence, helping them to maintain their relationship with the recipient.

It may be a heavy burden to bear, but companies that deliver gifts well can win in more ways than one. When a gift recipient opens a package from, say, Tiffany's—which (naturally!) presents gifts in its signature turquoise box and white ribbon that sets hearts aflutter with its symbolism of elegance and luxury, or from Pottery Barn, which wraps items so beautifully they seem to have come straight from the heart, instead of straight from a warehouse—a company is making good on the expectations of the giver by delivering delight to the recipient.

Not only do the giftees express their pleasure to the givers—who then feel all the more loyal to the company that delivered on its promise so well—but recipients of well-packaged gifts may love the presentation so much that they'll shop from that company themselves. So both retention *and* acquisition can be accomplished in one elegant tie of a ribbon and careful packaging of a shipment. Screw it up, though, and you could lose both an existing customer and a potential customer—so the trap is set for failure just as much as the opportunity is ripe for success.

Likewise, even before the box arrives at the door, delivery means following through with everything from easy order-tracking (by phone or online) to well-packaged (not overpackaged) shipments that are clearly branded with your company's name or logo (anonymous packages are a no-no in this age of anthrax).

Calling customers with an ETA, if they have to be home to receive delivery or installation, is another smart move. That's what Midwestern appliance retailer H. H. Gregg does, with its "40-minute Call-ahead Delivery" promise: Their drivers phone customers at home, office, or on their cell phones to let them know they're on the way. H. H. Gregg, which was also a pioneer in the field of same-day delivery, heavily promotes its call-ahead promise on everything from delivery trucks to television ads. While it may sound like a common courtesy, in a world where every consumer has a waiting-at-home horror story, it's a smart and consumer-centric point of differentiation.

H. H. Gregg further cements customer satisfaction through an in-stock guarantee, which kicks in if an advertised item is sold out. Customers get an upgrade to an even better product for the advertised price of the lesser item, instead of being stuck with only a rain check or an apology in lieu of what they had come to buy.

THE VOICE OF THE CUSTOMER
KEEP YOUR PROMISES.

A deal is a deal. If you made a promise, I expect you to stick to it. Low prices, high quality, speedy service—whatever your claim may be, live up to it. That also means that if you show "in stock" on your Web site, don't take my money and then tell me hours (or days!) later that you were mistaken and my order will be delayed, back-ordered, or canceled. This is misleading and inconvenient. Chances are I wouldn't have placed the order in the first place if I knew it was point-less. And show up on time when we have an appointment. Don't make me take a morning off from work only to have me sit around wondering if you'll make an appearance. Set a time and stick to it, if you want me to stick with you.

In a multichannel world, another series of postpurchase pitfalls emerges when companies fail to integrate their processes so that consumers can return or exchange, or seek service and support in every channel, no matter where the initial purchase or contact was made. Operating your channels like separate businesses and putting up barriers to cross-channel interaction will only confuse your customers and make you look like you don't have your act together. Giving them the seamless feel of one brand, one company, one experience will make your consumers see you as more well rounded and more accessible, even when they're not in immediate need of your products or services.

The postpurchase period, both short and long term, is about open communications. And not just from you. Give your customers a way to complain, compliment, query, or comment on their experiences, and respond, if necessary, swiftly and respectfully. If they're not making any noise, ask them to by actively seeking their advice to improve the way you do business with them and for them.

Systematic consumer feedback programs, in the form of surveys, review boards, or other ways of inviting input from your consumers, is worthwhile only if your company is committed to evolving as a result of that feedback. So don't treat surveys or consumer panels as just a way to head off complaints by letting consumers blow off steam; you've got to meet their issues head-on, not hide your head in the sand. If those forms go straight into the paper shredder without being read and reacted to, you won't be learning from the very people who have the most to teach you about your performance: your consumers.

Postpurchase elements that fall into categories already covered in **Exceed my Expectations** (Demandment Eight) and **Reward Me** (Demandment Nine)—such as following up with a thank-you note, or offering a small gift or reward along with an incentive to return—are also smart ways of showing consumers you still care about their business even after the transaction has been completed and the post-purchase phase is winding down.

✳ THE VOICE OF THE CUSTOMER
GIVE ME AN OUT.

Although we're developing a relationship, I sometimes have this queasy feeling that you're just stringing me along for the sake of my money. If you want me to commit to a long-term service agreement for say, a health-club membership or a time-share, make sure you give me a way out if I change my mind or want to change my level of commitment. I might actually want more, not less, from you, but either way, don't lock me in with stiff penalties that make me feel trapped. Once I've joined up, I expect an ongoing level of service and commitment that reflects my commitment to you. After I sign on I expect more, not less from you, so don't make me regret my decision by letting the line go dead on this long-term connection.

Once the postpurchase period has passed, the quiet time begins. Now, while consumers may not be thinking of you, you still need to be thinking of them and advocating for them. This is the time when you have the chance to improve your standing: when your consumer isn't standing in front of you.

This quiet period is all about innovation and continuity. The cogs should always be turning behind the scenes at your company, and that means researching consumer needs and developing new products, services, and capabilities to improve your brand experience; and all the while, you also should be evolving and evangelizing the consumer-centric behaviors within your company that keep the gears oiled and the muscles flexed to serve your consumers.

Some companies are in an almost perpetual variation of this mode: so richly infused in their customers lives that there's never either a quiet or a noisy period but rather a sort of subterranean buzz that vibrates in the background, humming along every day of their lives without beginning or ending. These iconic brands, like Coca-Cola, Disney, and McDonald's, are so deeply infused into popular culture, lifestyle, and society that their presence in people's lives goes beyond the tactical touchpoints of actual consumer transactions. They seep into the nooks and crannies of our world, as much institutions as they are brands.

Iconic brands are built on the legacy of long-term emotional connections of the kind we discussed in the Second Demandment

ICONIC BRANDS ARE BUILT ON THE LEGACY OF LONG-TERM EMOTIONAL CONNECTIONS.

chapter, **Inspire Me**. But you can't rely on memory alone to stoke those fires—which is why even such mega-brands, perhaps more than all others, must seek to engage their consumers in new or involving ways, or risk losing their cultural eminence.

Product development oriented toward changing consumer needs, and riding the waves of consumer tastes and trends, is one way to keep these brands freshly inserted into people's lives. Another way is by creating experiences that turn the brand's culture into a destination in and of itself—whether physical or virtual—one that immerses consumers in the brand experience through interactivity and entertaining information.

While the Web offers plenty of interactive ways for companies to share their history and culture with consumers (check out the Virtual Coke Factory tour at their corporate site, for one great example), the most immersive experiences are still real ones.

Whether you are welcoming visitors into a factory tour, company history museum, or entertainment experience, when you make your brand a physical destination for consumers you make it larger than life and bigger than their sum of its products in their eyes.

Visitors to the free Chocolate World attraction in Hershey, Pennsylvania, for instance, can take a theme-parklike ride through the story of chocolate-making (and then end up in a gift shop filled with sweet treats). Likewise, fun and fact-filled company museums and visitor's centers, like the one recently opened by Hormel to

HERSHEY'S: THE SWEETEST BRAND ON EARTH

Hershey's chocolate is one of those persistent, persuasive brands that stay with consumers even after they've thrown away the wrappers or exercised off those extra calories. This sweetest of brands has turned a simple, inexpensive product into a legacy, a destination, and an experience—and won the spare change and devoted taste buds of generations of Americans.

From the Hershey Kisses wrapped in colored foil to match every holiday and season, to the world-class spa at The Hotel Hershey (in Hershey, Pennsylvania), where guests can enjoy whipped cocoa baths and chocolate fondue wraps, Milton Hershey's chocolate company has become a multidimensional brand experience with no beginning or end in the lives of its customers.

Mr. Hershey began laying the groundwork at the end of the nineteenth century, and today his legacy still prospers and grows ever richer in the hands of folks like Milton Matthews, Hershey Food Corp.'s Vice President and Chief Customer Officer. "Innovation not only builds the category but it also helps drive the established brands just through the excitement. So innovations can be anything. Innovate on seasons. On packaging. On placement."

The mere fact that people can't pay for groceries, gas, hardware, or rental videos without being tempted by a Hershey Bar or a Reese's Peanut Butter Cup is a testament to the pervasiveness of the brand. But take a jaunt to the company's hometown of Hershey, Pennsylvania—"The Sweetest Place On Earth"SM—and you'll see that the brand doesn't just have legs, it has a life, and a landscape, all its own.

You know it the moment you arrive in downtown Hershey: The street lamps resemble Hershey's Kisses (alternating between wrapped and unwrapped), and the air is delicately scented with the aroma of, yes, chocolate. Visitors can stroll along Chocolate and Cocoa Avenues, enjoy the rides and attractions of HERSHEYPARK and Hershey Gardens, explore the company's history at the Hershey Museum, and enjoy elegant accommodations at the Hotel Hershey. And of course, no tour of this cocoa community is complete without a stop at the free Chocolate World Visitors' Center, for a simulated factory-tour ride and some free samples of Hershey's products.

For Milton Matthews, the place, the brand, and the idea are all one and the same. And the mouth-watering pleasure of the experience is just good business. "We have a very simple saying," he explains. "You see candy. You buy candy. You eat candy. And it keeps going on and on."

promote its Spam™ brand, or traveling icons, such as the Oscar Meyer WienerMobile™ or the Goodyear blimp, build strong nostalgic connections with customers by giving them more intimate access to the brands and products they've grown up with, or grown to love.

Staying with consumers also means that your consumers stay with you, in the form both of their data and (one hopes) of their actual business, driving your company ever forward toward better service and finer experiences. Even if you've had limited contact with your customers, anything at all that you know about them becomes the lifeblood of your business, flowing through your company's circulatory system. So whether you have a wealth of data on individuals—from personal profiles and buying patterns to contact logs and satisfaction surveys—or just a generalized picture of what's selling and what's not—the long-term relationships you forge with customers will be built on the foundation of knowledge you've gleaned over time about their wants, needs, and demands.

As Scott Smith, Vice President of eBusiness and Global Brand for Ford's TH!NK Mobility, notes, "It's a long way from knowing what people have bought in the past to being able to migrate them to purchases in the future. The problem [with data mining] is that it takes a lot longer than you'd like it to take, and we tend to focus on the sale. How do we market them their next car? Now how do we make them an advocate of our product? And once we make consumers advocates, they'll buy the next car."

> ONCE WE MAKE CONSUMERS ADVOCATES, THEY'LL BUY THE NEXT CAR.
>
> **Scott Smith, Ford Motor Co.**

Building this evolving foundation of consumer understanding—often through some of the calls-to-action defined in Demandment Seven, **Get to Know Me**—is the invisible activity that should always be in play at your company, no matter where you are in the transaction cycle. But you also have to be subtly visible to your customers at all times, and this is especially true during this quiet period. The old saying, "Out of sight, out of mind," is a simple but real reminder that you need to find creative, nonintrusive, and meaningful ways to stay with your consumers for the long haul.

THE VOICE OF THE CUSTOMER
KEEP UP WITH ME.

Life goes on, as they say—including mine. I may have moved on since we last connected. A new house, new city, new job, new spouse, new baby, new tastes, or a just a new outlook on life. But if all you do to stay in touch with me is send out an annual holiday card, I'm not feeling very connected to you, so you've got a lot of catching up to do.

Here's how to keep things going. . . .

- **Accept my updates.** You make it difficult to keep in touch, and sometimes it feels like there's no single person or place where I can update you about my life. Your associates move, quit, or are laid off. Your Web site only cares about where to send a package. So create a way for me to keep you up-to-date with my life, what I like and what I want from you.

- **Check in.** Ask me if something is new, different, important, or on my mind. A phone call or an email, if I've told you it's okay, or a survey in your store or on your Web site will do. Don't wait to hear from me until I'm surfacing a complaint or hunting you down after you've disappeared. You don't want that, and I certainly don't want it either. Checking in with me shows you're sincere when you say you want to keep up with my life.

- **See me as I am.** Don't try to make me into something I'm not, or force-fit me into some generic group just because of where I live or how old I am. See me for whom I really

am, not whom you think I am. If I don't make a ton of
money, don't try to sell me a car, house, or investment I
can't really afford. And if I've experienced some changes
in my life, work with me to help me see what that means,
and stay with me as I work through what I need from you.

Great models for ongoing consumer relationships are all around
you, and they're closer to home than you realize. Consider the dentist you grew up visiting as a kid; your children's pediatrician; your
family veterinarian; or the local ice cream parlor that's been a part of
your life for as long as you can remember. That's what the extended-
play side of **Stay with Me** is all about: being a part of people's
worlds in such an interwoven, holistic way that even when they
don't need you, they think of you as a part of their lives.

Think about your high school or college alumnae association for a
minute. Sure, they're helping to keep the fundraising spigots open
for the school; the greatest service they provide to former classmates,
however, is simply that of serving as a way for people to stay in
touch. From class reunions to job-placement assistance, alumni
magazines to school-sponsored lectures and tours, you'd be hard
pressed to find a better model for earning and keeping loyalty over
time than this sort of ultimate institutional memory organization.
Maybe that's why Classmates.com has been one of the most successful subscription services on the Internet—founded in 1995, by mid-
2001 the company had registered more than 6.5 million members,
some 350,000 of whom had paid $15 to $25 a piece for premier
services that gave them greater access to classmate-contact information and news.

Some business-to-consumer relationships are by their very nature
designed around a principle of long-term commitment, despite
intermittent interactions. Dentists and doctors, lawyers and

mechanics, hairdressers and dry cleaners—once people find one they like, chances are they'll stick with that provider for the long haul. But even professionals who have long depended on a steady clientele need to consider the changing landscape of consumer expectations, in which people no longer necessarily remain faithful to their providers unless they feel connected to them even between visits.

Likewise, certain service-provider brands such as AAA, which loyal members depend upon, year-in, year-out, for emergency roadside service and trip-planning resources, have been designed to remain a silent but constant companion in the consumers' lives, always at the ready when needed but never pushy when not called upon.

One of the newest and most successful entrants into this field of ever-present service brands is General Motors' OnStar, the in-vehicle telematics system that, on the most basic level, serves as a hands-free device for cellular phone calling. But while it may not be used as frequently, a cooler feature, marketed in a glitzy campaign featuring Batman, has garnered it the most attention: At the push of a button, OnStar drivers have access to emergency or roadside assistance and directional advice, so they're never really driving alone. That kind of always-at-your-side service stays with people no matter where they go. And that's a true loyalty-builder.

CUSTOMER LOYALTY SHOULD NEVER BE ASSUMED. IT MUST BE WON AGAIN AND AGAIN.

Customer loyalty should never be assumed. It must be won again and again, and the greatest battlefield for relationship-building is the wide-open spaces between interactions, where customers are free agents, open to wooing by other providers, brands, or services. While it may be easier (read: less demanding) for a customer to stay with his current barber or lawn-

❋ ONSTAR: ALWAYS ON, ALWAYS THERE

In recent years, American cars (with the exception of the Corvette, of course) have been considered somewhat stodgy in design and lacking in the creative technical touches found in many of their hipper foreign cousins. With the introduction of OnStar in 1996, however, General Motors surprised the competition (and the world) with a revolutionary driver-assistance service that's bringing new buyers to GM brands—and demonstrating the value of staying with the consumer long after a major purchase.

The OnStar in-car information-and-assistance service, which charges subscribers a monthly fee for access, not only offers a hands-free cellular phone system but connects drivers with live phone support for driving directions and roadside assistance. Drivers can even check their email on this whiz-bang system. Subscribers simply press one of three discrete buttons on their dashboard or rear-view mirror and use voice commands to request information or help.

As of the end of 2001, nearly two million drivers had subscribed to OnStar (doubling its subscriber total in just nine months). This rapid growth is not surprising, since this is the first system of its kind to actually live up to the promise of in-car information systems. And with an aging population concerned about safety and security, having OnStar onboard is as good as having a copilot in the passenger seat.

Behind OnStar's user-oriented simplicity is a sophisticated combination of GPS location technology, cellular communication, Internet resources, and live human customer service. Indeed, what we have here is the first established brand of "telematics," an emerging technology that enhances driving safety, security, and convenience. In the future, analysts predict, telematics will provide real-time engine diagnostics, downloadable music, Web browsing, and more.

The company aggressively markets OnStar via a cinematic, special-effects-laden Batman-theme TV campaign that's reinforced with comiclike demos on its Web site. This interesting approach seems to be paying off—for while Batman doesn't align with OnStar's older, Cadillac-driving initial audience, it may be pushing the buttons of all those younger, gadget-craving buyers who are beginning to raise families and think about automotive safety in a whole new light.

OnStar's limitation to GM-only brands may have caused it to hit a glass ceiling in terms of market share for subscribers; but General Motors has begun working with other auto-makers, including Lexus and Acura, to extend its reach into other car brands. That's a smart move, given that Verizon has announced that a similar automated calling and assistance system, called Wingcast, is poised for introduction into Ford and Nissan vehicles in 2002.

Though the cool factor certainly turns heads (especially those dreaming of driving a souped-up, plugged-in surfing machine), there can be no doubt that telematics systems such as OnStar's are the biggest thing to happen to auto safety since the development of the airbag. Cars with OnStar on-board can call for help in case of an accident (and help rescuers pinpoint a vehicle's location via GPS) even if the driver is too injured to push a call button. And with a growing number of states banning hand-held cellular calls, the hands-free communications system could well become standard in new cars within a few years.

But perhaps OnStar's greatest success has come with its ability to create a sense of a continuing relationship between carmaker and car-owner. That feeling may not last, of course, once drivers begin to think of the in-car information system as just another disembodied tool; but for now, GM's OnStar system remains so closely associated with its manufacturer that drivers feel as if the emblem on the hood represents the helpful voice on the other end of the line.

care company, if a new barbershop opens up with great new services or specials, or a neighbor's lawn looks amazingly good and he recommends another company to your own customer, then suddenly your customer has wandered off the ranch and into the next farmer's paddock.

That's why, in an age where consumers expect to be wined and dined, or at least teased and pleased, it's not enough to send a reminder postcard when it's getting close to the time for that next checkup or oil change. You've got to stay with your customer during those down times and show that because you know them and care about them, you've always got their best interests in mind.

Whether we're talking about the corner mechanic or a multinational computer company, understanding how consumers and businesses connect over time is critical to the long-term success of those relationships. Alex Sozonoff, Vice President of Customer Advocacy for Hewlett-Packard, says his team coined the term "Total Customer

> WE SAID, "OKAY, LET'S CREATE A FANTASTIC EXPERIENCE AS THE CUSTOMER GETS THE BOX." THAT'S CALLED THE "OUT-OF- BOX" EXPERIENCE.
>
> **Alex Sozonoff,**
> **Hewlett-Packard**

Experience" (TCE) when they were seeking to understand how consumers interact with their brand through the course of a typical relationship lifecycle, from the first phase—how a customer initially comes into contact with the brand—through the purchase process and on to the delivery phase, when the customer receives the product, and beyond. Sozonoff says the delivery phase was one of the TCE moments his team really focused on. "We said, 'Okay, Let's create a fantastic experience as the customer gets the box.' That's called the 'out-of-box' experience."

Sozonoff's team also focused on making sure that everything from simple set-up instructions to helpful call-center support was in place, so that the out-of-the-box experience launched HP consumers into an easy and uneventful installation and learning process. "And then you have the replacement products," Sozonoff adds, as the TCE continues its course. "We actually closed the loop, so we created the Total Customer Experience benchmark around a circle."

This kind of cyclical thinking helps keep companies in the loop of their consumers' lives, in between sales and over the course of time. Often, companies use relevant communications as the tool of when keeping a line open to their consumers' lives—offering valuable information that doesn't sell products so much as enrich their use.

A quarterly newsletter filled with tips, ideas, reminders, and to-do lists can work for almost any kind of business: from pet food stores to yoga studios, groceries to pediatricians. It's a great way to keep customers informed while also letting them know you care. Don't spam your customers with constant communications; rather let them know a few times a year, at relevant moments (such as spring-cleaning time, for a household appliance company, or flea season, for a veterinarian) that you're keeping in mind what's going on in their lives as the year goes by. Add value to your communications and you add meaning to your relationship.

People are inundated with unwanted communications as it is. So making sure these newsletters or other contacts are wanted, by having peo-

THE GREATEST BATTLEFIELD FOR RELATIONSHIP-BUILDING IS THE WIDE-OPEN SPACES BETWEEN INTERACTIONS.

ple actively sign up for them (or opt in, on a Web site), will heighten the likelihood that they'll actually be read when they come in over the often overcrowded transom of daily mail and email.

Ubiquitous mega-brands, including Coca-Cola, Nike, and Ford, have been investing more heavily in custom-publishing ventures in recent years, producing magazinelike publications that soft-sell their marketing messages while targeting their audiences' interests. Ford's *No Boundaries* quarterly contains rugged driving content that makes readers want to head for the great outdoors (in their Ford SUVs, of course), while Nike's *NikeGoddess* publication serves up lifestyle and wellness articles tailored to a fit female audience. These publications are a cross between info-tainment and adver-to-rial, which makes them . . . well . . . informative adver-tainment, infused as they are with well-targeted attitudes and lifestyle associations, and with topical features aimed at already receptive audiences, these iconic brands don't need to sell through this medium so much as continue to insert themselves into their loyalists' lives in fresh and engaging ways.

The insurance industry relies on these sorts of interim communications (though some agencies do it better than others), in part because what it sells is all about what happens between transactions. People buy insurance hoping that they *won't* need it—and when they do, it's rarely planned. So, for instance, when the Farmers Insurance Group provides its policyholders with its 24/7 HelpPoint® assistance—on-call advisers who can help people over the hump of emergencies large and small—they're showing their customers that they're always there for them, no matter when, no matter where. And not only when it's time to renew policies.

Following consumers down the natural trail of their lives, through the stages of youth, young adulthood, middle age, and the later years creates a predictive path for many kinds of products and services. And those companies that understand how the natural series of life events—going to college, getting married, having a baby, changing jobs, retiring, etc.—plays itself out in their consumers' lives are the ones that have the best chance of hanging in there with consumers all the way through the process. Insurance companies, banks, and other financial institutions are particularly adept at using life-stages to develop and market products and services that reflect the changing needs of their customers.

THE VOICE OF THE CUSTOMER
BE THERE FOR ME.

Be there when I need you. With new, innovative products that take my life better. A great location, close to home and work. A readily accessible operator, with helpful tips and with answers to my toughest questions. Have policies that look out for my interests. And a reliable Web site and product warranties. All of it. But most important, be there in attitude. Show me that I'm important by reaching out, following through, and simply caring, after my purchase. We'll both be glad you did.

As the demographics of the overall population changes, however—as it ages, plans for retirement, and begins to pass along its wealth to the subsequent generations—this cultural shift offers opportunities for brands to extend their consumer relationships in new directions. Whether that means marketing roomier exercise clothes to accommodate middle-aged spread, or developing senior daycare services to assist adult children in caring for their aging parents, changes in demographic life-cycles spotlight ways for companies to reinvent their relevancy to their consumers' lives.

Being innovative and responsive in the ways you seek to stay with your consumers is a key to making your relationship with them meaningful. And this means not only staying with them during the changes in their lives, but also being with them where they live.

So stage unique events that bring the community together, like a parking-lot dog wash to benefit the local humane society, or a post-holiday gift-away party, where people can donate unwanted gifts to local charities. Find ways to celebrate the things that matter to you and your customers—through special sales where the proceeds go to local schools, or by staging or sponsoring athletic competitions, arts festivals, or other events that keep your brand in tune with the things that matter to the community at large and to your consumers in particular. Don't just open your doors in the morning and close them at night; think of your brand, and your business, as always involved, always infused, always interjected into the lives and lifestyles of your customers, and they'll feel like you're there with them all the time, too.

WHEN YOU'RE
CLOSE TO YOUR
CONSUMERS, GOOD
THINGS HAPPEN.

**Paul Charron,
Liz Claiborne**

"When you're close to your consumers, good things happen," says Paul Charron, CEO of Liz Claiborne. And while it seems like such a simple statement, it goes to the heart of every great relationship between companies and consumers.

In the end, to get your consumers to stay with you you've got to stay close enough to them to be able to view their interactions with you as part of a longer continuum, as opposed to mere isolated events. Many of the ideas embedded in the Ten Demandments—from inspiration to rewards, guidance to access—are fluid elements of an experience-stream that winds and flows farther than the eye can see.

Following through by keeping these experiences clear, compelling, relevant, and reliable, no matter whether consumers are standing on the riverbanks or floating in midstream, will keep them engaged with your company over time. And the companies that stay with their consumers as they flow along through life will discover that, in a classic sense, the journey really is its own reward.

DEMANDMENT 10: **STAY WITH ME—SELF-EVALUATION**

Now that you've read this Demandment, see how you stack up. The checkpoints in this form reflect the key takeaways from the "Voice of the Customer" sections. Identify where your company could stand some improvement, and you'll have a shot at building bridges with the people who keep you in business.

10. STAY WITH ME	Excellent	Good	Poor
It's not over 'til it's over.	Make returns hassle-free, including gift returns, and issue immediate credit.	Accept merchandise returns, including gifts.	Move on immediately after the transaction.
Keep your promises.	Make promises for follow-through that are kept and guaranteed—always, across all channels.	Make promises for follow-through that are kept and guaranteed—always.	Promises are not guaranteed.
Give me an out.	Clearly communicate to customers easy options for canceling transaction or relationship with company.	Let consumers cancel transaction or relationship with company, if necessary.	Don't accept cancellations.
Keep up with me.	Provide a way for consumers to easily update their information or file complaints or suggestions.	Occasionally get in touch with consumers to verify their information, see if they have concerns or suggestions.	Don't check in with consumers.
Be there for me.	Evolve to meet customers' ongoing needs through innovative products and unrelenting helpfulness.	Always ready with unrelenting helpfulness.	Relationship is weakened between transactions.

Index

INDEX